Oscar Wilde

Oscar Wilde

Sheridan Morley

PAVILION

Paperback edition published in Great Britain in 1997 by
PAVILION BOOKS LIMITED
26 Upper Ground, London SE1 9PD

Hardback edition published in Great Britain in 1976 by
Weidenfeld & Nicolson

A CIP catalogue record for this book is available
from the British Library.

ISBN 1 86205 034 1

Printed in Great Britain by Hartnolls, Bodmin

2 4 6 8 10 9 7 5 3 1

This book can be ordered direct from the publisher. Please contact
the Marketing Department. But try your bookshop first.

For Sewell Stokes, my godfather,
co-author of the first English play about Wilde,
and for Robert and Joan, my parents,
who met on account of that play.

CONTENTS

PREFACE

*Nothing can be more absurdly untrue than the assertion which is invariably made
by about half the reviewers when a new book about Wilde comes out – that the
subject is exhausted and that nobody wants to hear any more about it. The subject
will never be exhausted, just precisely because of its human and dramatic interest.*

Lord Alfred Douglas, 1937.

But what is that human and dramatic interest? The story of Oscar Wilde has
usually been told in terms of *hubris* – Oscar as the child of the gods, lavishly
endowed with every talent except that of restraint, whom they destroyed because
that's the kind of thing gods do.

In fact, there is a more prosaic explanation of Wilde's theatrical triumphs and
of his social collapse: he was a child not of the gods but of the Victorians, and his
tragedy was that he allowed himself to remain one.

Like all children he failed to recognize or to estimate the moment at which the
grown-ups would stop laughing. Like Peter Pan (created only four years after
Wilde's death) rather than Icarus, he refused to age or to take stock of his
surroundings and for that the Victorians broke him: his crimes were crimes
against their admittedly ambiguous concept of a decent society, and when he
reached the witness box for the last time he was like a man in the wrong suit at
the wrong party, only then realizing that he did not have the social or political
strength to get away with it.

One of the greater tragedies – well, misfortunes really, but something about
Oscar encourages one to exaggerate – of Wilde's life was that he and television
missed each other by about fifty years. If ever a man was made for the instant
fame of the chat show it was surely Oscar, whose finest achievement was not his
poetry, nor yet his one novel, nor even his children's stories, but his conversation
and the four comedies in which he recorded the best of it for posterity. That he
was a great playwright (arguably the best in the language after Shakespeare and
Shaw) is still largely unchallenged, but it is a reputation which rests purely on
language, since his plots and his characterizations were on his own admission
inclined to be a little sketchy. What interested Oscar, in much the same way as it
interested another Irishman, Brendan Behan, was the sound of the language.

Wilde was not the last of an historical line stretching back to Sheridan and Congreve, and with Bernard Shaw he had little in common beyond a place and rough date of birth; instead, Oscar was the founding father of a sound-oriented group of writers whose membership was later to include O'Casey and Behan and Dylan Thomas.

But what follows is not literary criticism, nor yet another attempt to right the wrongs of some previous Wilde biographies; just as Oscar's later life was riddled with litigation, so for almost fifty years after his death it seemed impossible for anyone to write a book about him without at least one other author leaping into print to refute it. Oscar-writers were divided into two main groups: those who saw him as a great betrayed genius and those who saw him as a raging and tiresome 'old queen' who got what was coming to him and none too soon. In the three-quarters of a century since his death the pendulum has swung first one way and then back the other, and hopefully it may now at last be coming to rest somewhere in the middle.

This book, then, is not a thesis but an attempt at hardback documentary – an attempt to show that Oscar's own life was indeed the greatest of all his theatrical productions and one in which the ending was as inevitable as the horror of Lady Bracknell when she discovers John Worthing's connection with a handbag at Victoria Station. The final test of Wilde as a playwright lies in that scene, and the fact that it still works on any stage anywhere in the world; a lesser playwright would almost certainly have disappeared forever under the weight of the scandal, a weight which the passing of eighty years has done curiously little to alleviate. The smug postwar theory has been that we have grown up since Oscar's time, and that his fate could never be repeated: the fact remains however that many of the offences with which he was charged are still technically and actually punishable by imprisonment since they involved minors, and the subject or even the suggestion of homosexuality in public life retains a kind of amazed fascination of the type once reserved for men who admitted a working knowledge of marijuana or who sent children down the mines.

But to understand what really happened to Oscar Wilde it is important to understand the world in which he lived; by no means the cloistered, poetic hothouse in which early biographers were keen to place him, it was instead the commercial theatre and publishing worlds of London in the 1880s and early nineties. Like Frank Harris (who, typically, was among the first to make a speedy sovereign out of the trials, but with whom Wilde had more in common than many would admit), Oscar had a journalist's sense of occasion: a shrewd self-publicist with an eye for the headlines, Wilde left only one real mystery behind him. How could anyone with so well-developed a sense of his own image and of the importance of preserving it have failed to see the trap he was getting himself into until it was too late? That is the fundamental question of this book, and to answer it we have to go back to the very beginning.

1
AN IRISH
CHILDHOOD

—

1854–1874

It would, I suppose, be over-optimistic to expect Oscar Wilde to have come of ordinary parentage: just as nothing in his life became him like the leading of it, so everything about him dating back even to his parents' generation hovered around the borders of eccentricity. Consider his father, for instance: Sir William Wilde was, in his later life, Surgeon Oculist in Ordinary to Her Britannic Majesty Queen Victoria, which meant presumably that if ever she had any eye trouble while in Ireland he was her man. He was also a Fellow of the Royal College of Surgeons and somewhat less than meticulous about his appearance, which is why one of the best-known and most often quoted jokes about him ran: 'Why are Dr Wilde's nails so black? Because he will keep scratching himself.'

Already, therefore, we are in a realm of suspended disbelief: if only he could have managed a hunchback, or maybe a stammer as well, the innumerable Wildean biographies already published would have rather more enthralling opening chapters. It is indeed ironic that the only widely-known life of Sir William should be entitled *The Parents of Oscar Wilde*, since by any standards of publicity lesser than Oscar's, Sir William would surely have merited a book in his own sole right. For his was, by any accounting, a remarkable if somewhat unkempt career: born in 1815, the third son of a country doctor, he was sent by his Anglo-Irish parents from Roscommon to Dublin, where at the age of seventeen he began studying to be a surgeon. While still a student he diagnosed an unsuspected case of cholera during a stay with some relatives in Connaught, nursed the patient through to his death, and then fumigated his home to prevent the epidemic spreading. Subsequently a wealthy patient took him to Egypt, where he first studied trachoma and began the ophthalmic research which was to result in an eventually lucrative Dublin practice and his appointment to the Queen.

In the meantime, in 1851 he had married Jane Francesca Elgee, the granddaughter of an Archdeacon of Wexford, and herself by this time a 'parlour Fenian', poetess and avowed Irish Nationalist writing under the name of 'Speranza'. Never scrupulous about the date of her birth (she often gave it as 1826, which would have been all right had not her father's records indicated that he in fact died in 1824), Jane was, in Terence de Vere White's view, 'a tragic figure in whom journalists were apt to see comic possibilities'. A large, militant lady married to a small and not physically lovely man, she and her husband had all the makings of a comic vaudeville team sent on to do the warm-up for Oscar. Yet in her time, Speranza had a considerable following for her poetry, and her own career had a suitably dramatic beginning. Born, let us charitably assume, in 1824 and brought up quietly by her mother in Wexford, she was one day watching the funeral in Dublin of a nationalist poet named Thomas Davis. Years later, on his 1882 lecture tour of America, Oscar set the scene:

Standing at the window of her lordly house, she saw a great funeral pass in its solemn trappings of sorrow down the street and followed by crowd after crowd of men and women in bitter and unrestrained grief. Wondering what man had died whom the people so loved, she asked who it was they were burying and learned it was the funeral of one Thomas Davis, a poet of whom until then she had never heard. That evening she bought and read his poems and knew for the first time the meaning of the word country.

She also knew then and there, if Oscar is to be believed, that she too had to be a nationalist poet, and apart from the fact that the 'lordly house' was actually a maisonette in Lower Leeson Street, Oscar seems accurate in his account of his mother's sudden determination. 'Oh!' she was soon writing:

... for a hundred thousand muskets glittering brightly in the light of heaven and the monumental barricades stretching across each of our noble streets made desolate by England – circling round that doomed Castle, where the foreign tyrant has held his council of treason and iniquity against our country and our people for seven hundred years ... One bold, one decisive move. One instant to take breath, and then a rising; a rush, a charge from north, south, east and west upon the English garrison, and the land is ours.

The Dublin paper for which Speranza wrote that, *Nation*, was however rapidly suppressed by the English and its editor Gavan Duffy sent to prison. Speranza herself had the grace to admit at his trial: 'I alone am the culprit' but the occupying authorities, thinking twice perhaps about the wisdom of imprisoning a woman, and an increasingly well-known one at that, left her in freedom to continue her writing – prose and verse more remarkable, admittedly, for its passion than for its artistry. But by now she had already befriended William Wilde, whom she had first encountered soon after writing an intensely favourable review of his essay on 'Irish Popular Superstitions' for the Dublin University magazine, and with their marriage she began for a while to fade into his shadow. Theirs was not, initially, a bad life: 'they rose together,' notes Martin Fido, 'from respectable Westland Row to fashionable Merrion Square; from brilliant youth to distinguished middle age; from Dr Wilde and Speranza to Sir William and Lady Wilde.'

Their first son, Willie, was born at 21 Westland Row towards the end of 1852; their second, patriotically christened Oscar Fingal O'Flahertie (he himself later added Wills), was born there too on 16 October 1854. There was also a third child, a daughter named Isola, born in 1856, who died soon after her tenth birthday, leaving the younger of her two brothers with a sorrow he never forgot. He wrote of her in 'Requiescat' (1881):

> Tread lightly, she is near
> Under the snow,
> Speak gently, she can hear
> The daisies grow.
>
> All her bright golden hair
> Tarnished with rust,
> She that was young and fair
> Fallen to dust.

A year or so after Oscar's birth the family moved up in the Dublin world to an elegant Georgian townhouse at 1 Merrion Square, and his parents, though still a curious couple (Bernard Shaw – born two years after Wilde, and only a few hundred yards away from Westland Row – was later to maintain that Speranza suffered from giantism, and even the otherwise restrained Lewis Broad is convinced that Dr Wilde 'shuffled about like an ape'), continued to thrive. Vyvyan Holland, the younger of Oscar's own two sons, while less sure about his grandparents' grotesque appearance, was sure that Speranza had been hoping for a girl when Oscar was born, and that she kept him in blue velvet dresses until the beginning of her third pregnancy. One early photograph of Oscar at two does bear this out, to the huge delight of countless subsequent professional and amateur analysts seeking a root cause for Oscar's subsequent sexual inclinations. On the other hand it should perhaps be remembered that many parents of the 1850s were in the habit of clothing all small children in long dresses in their earliest years.

William Wilde had many other children besides Speranza's; his medical partner Henry Wilson was in fact a natural son, and there were at least two illegitimate daughters, though probably not 'a bastard in every farmhouse', as his less charitable colleagues were ever eager to assert. Yet it says more than a little for Dr Wilde's talent and charisma that he was able to overcome a distinctly strange personal appearance and some distinctly nasty personal habits to become a leading figure in Dublin society. St John Ervine elaborates:

Undersized and ugly, he had the features of a ferret. His forehead was high and narrow, noble even, and full of intellectual authority, but his chin receded into his throat so sharply that it could hardly be called a chin: a mere lapse of flabby flesh into a dirty bush of beard. The mouth which hung above it was long and loose, the sort of mouth that slobbers in old age: a bestial and protruding mouth, especially in its lower lip, which was full of casual lust that can never be sated . . . he had strong, simian arms that hung heavily down his sides and seemed too long for his body: arms that would be prompt to crush. It was the simian look of him, simian in limbs more than in features, which first impressed those who met him. Yet there was a remarkable mind behind his animal head. The ape he resembled was struggling to become human and escape from the jungle.

Ten years after Oscar's birth came a remarkable double for his 'simian' father: Dr Wilde got his knighthood from Queen Victoria's Viceroy and within six months found himself enmeshed in a libel suit brought against his wife – a celebrated trial which was to find an uneasy parallel in Oscar's own life thirty years later. First the knighthood: though granted by a grateful Queen it was not in fact for Dr Wilde's many achievements as a surgeon (Her Majesty apparently never had any eye trouble while visiting Ireland) or as an archaeologist (another of the Doctor's many interests), but rather for 'Services to statistical science, especially in connexion with the Irish Census' which he had helped to administer.

A few months later, and because of the knighthood, one of Sir William's past *affaires* caught up with him. His fidelity to Speranza had always been somewhat shaky, even at the outset of their marriage, but with his increasing celebrity and the money it afforded her to run salons at which her love for Irish nationalist poetry and its writers could be indulged, she had chosen to turn a blind eye – after all, his affairs were a purely domestic matter, of concern only to himself and apparently known to few others except of course those who were intimately involved. One of the Doctor's 'friends' had however been Mary Josephine Travers, who in the year of Oscar's birth had gone to Dr Wilde for the treatment of an inflamed ear. She was then an attractive nineteen-year-old, and Dr Wilde, as was often his custom in such cases, had taken more than a professional interest in her. However when in 1861 he had grown tired and wanted to break off the affair, Mary had begun sending a series of anonymous letters to Speranza describing the Doctor as a spiteful old lunatic.

Dr Wilde, having failed to buy Mary off or send her to Australia (a plan she once endorsed but then rapidly abandoned, having travelled no further than Liverpool), simply told Speranza that Mary was to be ignored, since she was more than a little deranged. This was possibly true, although it is not clear whether Speranza also knew that her fury with Dr Wilde had some basis in reality. In any case the publicity which surrounded the Doctor's knighthood in 1864 brought another series of irate notes from Mary, as well as a pamphlet in which she described the rape of one 'Florence Boyle Price' by a 'Doctor Quilp'. So as to leave little uncertainty over 'Quilp's' true identity, Mary distributed her pamphlet outside the Metropolitan Hall in Abbey Street, where the newly-knighted Wilde was lecturing on 'Ireland Past and Present'.

To avoid the gathering storm, Lady Wilde took Willie, Oscar and Isola off to Bray for the summer, but Mary pursued her there. Able to stand it no longer, Lady Wilde then wrote an irate letter to the girl's father, who was Professor of Medical Jurisprudence, no less, at Trinity College Dublin:

Sir,

You may not be aware of the disreputable conduct of your daughter at Bray, where she consorts with all the low newspaper boys in the place employing them to disseminate offensive placards in which my name is given, and also tracts in which she makes it appear that she has had an intrigue with Sir William Wilde. If she chooses to disgrace herself it is not my affair, but as her object in insulting me is the hope of extorting money for which she has several times applied to Sir William Wilde with threats of more annoyance if not given, I think it right to inform you, as no threat of additional insult shall ever extort money from our hands. The wages of disgrace she has so basely treated for and demanded shall never be given her.

Jane F. Wilde

Travers allowed his daughter to 'find' the letter among his papers. She, seeing in it a chance to get even with her ex-lover and his wife, promptly sued Speranza for libel, claiming £2000 in damages and knowing that Sir William would be cited as co-defendant since by the Irish laws of the time he was legally responsible for the actions of his wife.

The case was heard in Dublin during December 1864. Oscar, by now ten, was in his first term at Portora Royal School in Enniskillen, and although he is unlikely to have heard the full details of the trial until some years afterwards it is conceivable that some of his own curious court behaviour three decades later was influenced by the chaos, confusion and odd disregard for any kind of truth at this first Wilde trial. For in Dublin in 1864, as in London in 1895, the motives of those involved on either side of the case were so convoluted, and so far removed from what their owners thought or professed them to be, that the trial's outcome was more a matter of luck than judgment.

Mary's own counsel told the court the predictable tale of a poor nineteen-year-old innocent seduced by her evil doctor, but cross-examination soon established that she could not even remember the day on which it happened.

'Did you,' asked counsel for Lady Wilde, 'tell anyone of what had taken place?'
'No.'
'Not even your father?'
'No.'
'Why not?'

'I did not wish to give him pain.'

'But you went back to Dr Wilde's study after this awful assault?'

'Yes.'

'You went again and again, did you not?'

'Yes.'

'Did he ever attempt to repeat the offence?'

'Yes.'

'And after the second offence you went back?'

'Yes.'

'Did he ever repeat it again?'

'Yes.'

That much established, defence counsel then put Lady Wilde under oath and she proceeded to deny all allegations that her husband and Mary had slept together at all. The jury thus had three totally contradictory stories presented to them within as many hours: first that Mary had been raped, second that she had been Sir William's willing lover, and third that she had not slept with him at all. Reaching the not unnatural conclusion that both Mary and Lady Wilde were lying their heads off, the jury decided that libel had been proved but that they would only award Mary a derisory farthing in damages, thereby neatly displaying for all their distrust if not their actual dislike of both plaintiff and defendant.

Sir William himself, realizing perhaps that his reputation as a distinguished surgeon was bound to suffer whichever way the case went, declined to appear in court at all. He did however pay a greater price than either Speranza or Mary Travers, one far above and beyond even the £2000 that the case set him back in costs: his scientific reputation remained intact, but he himself had little choice but to drop swiftly out of all Dublin society, spending more and more time at his Moytura country home. Rumour and truth had by now established him in roughly equal measure as a decidedly sinister fellow, and his private life was marked by a series of subsequent tragedies. Two years after the trial his legitimate daughter died, and a few years after that two of his natural daughters were burnt to death when one had her dress catch fire at a ball and the other tried unsuccessfully to save her.

Sir William died in the spring of 1876, when Oscar was just twenty-one, but for more than half the son's lifetime the father had been an increasingly shadowy figure, content to leave his upbringing in the hands of the Portora schoolmasters and the redoubtable Speranza – though St John Ervine, who made something of a study of the physical and mental peculiarities of Wilde's parents, reckoned that she was not much better than Sir William:

She was tall, like her second son, six feet in height, and is said to have been handsome despite her sallow skin, which seemed always to be bilious and sallow grey – another physical characteristic she shared with Oscar. It was this muddy look which made her plaster her face with paint and powder and sit in darkened rooms in the hope that make-up might be mistaken for the vitality she aped. She is reputed to have been a brilliant conversationalist, but the samples of her wit which have been preserved do not support this reputation; and in her last years she was ridiculous. People went to her salons, to see the sights: the faked old woman and her faked sons.

The first of Oscar's innumerable letters to his mother (like his others, all carefully annotated and arranged for posterity by Sir Rupert Hart-Davis) comes from Portora and is dated 8 September 1868. It indicates that his mother was still fervently intent on publishing her poems: 'Darling Mama, The hamper came today, I never got such a jolly surprise, many thanks for it, it was more than kind of you to think of it ... You never told me anything about the publisher in Glasgow, what does he say? And have you written to Aunt Warren on the green note paper?'

But Oscar was not happy at Portora: overshadowed by a more popular and outgoing elder brother, he was a bookish boy who, in the view of his own younger son:

... had little in common with other boys, as he disliked games and fighting and took more interest in flowers and sunsets than he did in the possession of knives and other objects treasured by most small boys. And he seems to have preferred his own company to that of his school-fellows, a preference which they seem to have reciprocated. He heartily disliked mathematics and anything to do with science. Indeed, his opinion of his own scholastic attainments is well summed up in his own aphorism: 'Nothing that is worth knowing can be taught'. When he was bored with the subject of a lesson, he would try to lead the master into a digression by ingeniously worded questions which had nothing to do with the matter in hand. His main interests in scholarship were poetry and the classics, particularly Greek, for which he had an inordinate passion.

Little more is known about Oscar at Portora, though believers in the faintly supernatural were gratified to discover that when a later headmaster went to remove Oscar's name from a scroll of academic honours at the time of the celebrated trials the wood had already cracked in precisely that place. But ignorance of Wilde's schooldays did not deter the inimitable Frank Harris who, inspired by his usual financial troubles to cobble together a wildly implausible but often hugely entertaining 'biography' ten years after Oscar's death, came up with a touching little scene (as apparently 'recounted' to Frank by Oscar himself) set in a railway carriage as, at the end of one Portora term, Oscar parted from a schoolfriend:

'You must go now,' I [Oscar] said to him.
'Yes,' he replied, in a queer muffled voice, while standing with his hand on the door of the carriage. Suddenly he turned to me and cried:
'Oh, Oscar,' and before I knew what he was doing he had caught my face in his hot hands and kissed me on the lips. The next moment he had slipped out of the door and

was gone ... I sat there all shaken. Suddenly I became aware of cold, sticky drops trickling down my face – his tears. They affected me strangely. As I wiped them off I said to myself in amaze:

'This is love: this is what he meant – love' ... I was trembling all over. For a long while I sat, unable to think, all shaken with wonder and remorse.

There is however no reputable evidence of any kind to support that particular sequence of events, and though one or two later biographers of Wilde have been keen to establish his homosexuality as early as Portora it is unlikely that Oscar's schooldays were any queerer than those of most of his fellow-pupils. What is clear is that it was this early in his life that he began separating himself from the seething mass of others. Portora was a 'Royal' school, built originally to reinforce England's Protestant control in Ireland and therefore still in Oscar's time excluding virtually all Catholics. His life there appears to have been uneventful, though scholastically by no means unimpressive.

Away from school, the cherished youngest surviving child of a dominating mother and an increasingly reclusive father, Oscar's childhood seems to have been cast in a mould almost too psychologically perfect for what was later to become of him. Yet all we really know is that he was a theatrical child, given to lavish displays of temperament like those over the premature death of his sister, to whose Edgeworthstown grave he paid long and frequent visits. While his brother was becoming the kind of hearty all-rounder who would end his days as a Fleet Street drunk (all the Wilde family had a lavish gift for living out their own worst character-expectations), Oscar spent his time under the influence of Speranza – herself fast becoming the kind of 'stage' mother who would fulfil herself through her child – reading such lush romantic fiction as *Melmoth The Wanderer*, a novel by her uncle Charles Maturin, from whose title character Oscar would one day take a name when his own was no longer acceptable. There are also contemporary accounts of the young Wilde hearing banshees the night before a relative's death, and generally behaving as though auditioning for the lead in a Victorian novel about poetic Irish children.

The redoubtable St John Ervine is under no illusion that Oscar was an unsatisfactory child:

He was unpopular with his schoolmates, as a large, ungainly boy with inert habits and an unfortunate fluency in devising apt but acid nicknames is certain to be. His own, which annoyed him, was Grey Crow ... untidy, inclined to flop about, slovenly in both appearance and dress, with hands and face always in need of washing, and with nails showing signs of mourning, he made no deep impression on his fellows; and such impression as he did make was generally unfavourable. He was kind to small boys, to whom he told stories and played the piano. He read much, but was absolutely incapable of mathematics, which is no crime though it is a nuisance ... any forecast of distinction that might have been made about him then would probably have been derided. His mother's assertion that he was 'a wonderful boy' was, no doubt, regarded as the nonsense of a fond mamma.

For all that, Oscar was far from stupid; shortly before his seventeenth birthday he won an open scholarship to Trinity College, Dublin, gaining a 'Second Entrance' prize in Greek verse. Oscar's arrival at Trinity College was on 10 October 1871, a week before his seventeenth birthday. Privately his family life may have been more than a little unsettled, but publicly he was still the cherished younger son of a distinguished local breed. 'I am not anxious about Willie,' Lady Wilde had written to a friend some years earlier, 'he has a well-shaped head; but I expect simply extraordinary things of Oscar' – the Wildes were after all in the business of being extraordinary whenever possible.

Sir William had by now been consulted for his ocular knowledge by both the King of Sweden (after whom it was said Oscar had been named, though his mother had merely noted that the name was 'grand, misty and Ossianic') and Napoleon III, to say nothing of the Emperor Maximilian. Speranza meanwhile had been translating Dumas and running an increasingly eccentric weekly salon at which one of the guests was uncharitable enough to describe her as 'a tragedy queen in a suburban theatre'. Lady Wilde herself, asked to comment on the difficulties of her private life with Sir William and his many affairs, declared memorably: 'I soar above the miasmas of the commonplace,' a philosophy which her younger son was to inherit. Asked to play football for Portora he had informed a surprised schoolmaster: 'It is all very well as a game for rough girls, but hardly suitable for delicate boys'; it was already clear that if he had to take after one of his parents it would almost certainly be his mother. ('All women become like their mothers. That is their tragedy. No man does. That's his' – *The Importance of Being Earnest*, 1895.)

Wilde's life at Trinity College, Dublin, where he stayed from 1871 to 1874, yields little of future significance beyond the facts that he won many prizes for classics, including the Berkeley Gold Medal for Greek, and that he came under the considerable influence of John Pentland Mahaffy, then Professor of Ancient History (later Provost), whose obsession with all things Greek was transmitted to his adoring pupil Oscar. Mahaffy was, by the reckoning of Hesketh Pearson:

. . . an out-and-out social snob. That is, he would rather have sat down to a bad meal with a stupid aristocrat than to a good meal with an intelligent tradesman . . . he loved a lord, adored a duke and would have worshipped a prince . . . Oscar responded eagerly to the Mahaffy treatment. Already a humorous and vivacious talker, under his tutor he realized the possibilities of the gift. Already a lover of the Greek poets and historians, he quickly became a lover of everything Greek. Not disinclined by nature and upbringing to accept worldly values, he was soon initiated by Mahaffy into the mysteries of snobbery, and taught that superciliousness was a sign of good breeding.

But beyond the influence of Mahaffy (one which was to extend well into Wilde's later student years) what had Trinity College to offer? The scrupulous research of Rupert Croft-Cooke has revealed only that the young Wilde seems to have had a poor record for attending lectures in subjects other than classical antiquity, and that although a member of the college debating society he never actually spoke there. Yet an interesting eye-witness account of Oscar at Trinity emerged some years later and in a curious way; in 1882, while Wilde was on his much-publicized lecture tour of the United States, reports in local papers began to describe an affected aesthete with an odd habit of rhapsodizing over sunflowers. Living in Salt Lake City at the time was one Horace Wilkins, who had been a fellow-pupil of Wilde's at Trinity, and in an attempt to equate the latterday Wilde with the 'ungainly, overgrown, awkward moping lad' he remembered from ten years back, Wilkins came up with the following Trinity memoir:

One day a thing happened which seemed, as it were, to change the current of Wilde's life. He wrote a poem which he read at one of the class symposiums. It struck me as a beautiful thing, but when he had finished reading the bully of the class laughed sneeringly. I never saw a man's face light up with such savagery of hate as Wilde's. He strode across the room and standing in front of the man asked him by what right he sneered at his poetry. The man laughed again and Wilde slapped him across the face. The class interfered, but inside of an hour the crowd was out behind the college arranging for a fight. Wilde, in a towering rage, was ready to fight with howitzers if necessary, but the bully wanted to fight with nature's weapons. No one supposed that Wilde had a ghost of a show, but when he led out with his right it was like a pile-driver. He followed the surprised bully up with a half dozen crushers and that ended it. Talk about a chap being a 'pallid young man'! When I see these allusions in the newspapers I always think of his fighting qualities. I think he would make an ox shake his head and blink. Well, after that, Wilde's stock was high at Trinity. It seemed to put new ambition into him, and the next term found him at the head of all his classes. He seemed to be able to master everything he tackled.

Pugilism apart, Wilde's academic career at Trinity thrived very largely on victory, academic or otherwise: he became a Queen's Scholar (entitling him to free board and lodging and £20 a year) soon after his arrival. and his subsequent devotion to Mahaffy (himself a frequent visitor to Lady Wilde's salon) was repaid when the tutor acknowledged Oscar's 'improvements and corrections' in the preface to his book on *Social Life in Greece from Homer to Menander*. Beyond that, Oscar was again a somewhat unobtrusive pupil, again overshadowed by his big brother Willie, who had preceded him to Trinity and was again getting on better with the other students. Among the latter was Edward Carson, later to appear for the defence of Lord Queensberry at the first of the celebrated trials, at which Oscar seemed convinced (albeit wrongly) that their shared undergraduate life in Dublin would not make Carson any more well-disposed towards him. In fact it seems unlikely that Carson had formed any particular view of Oscar as an undergraduate. Vyvyan Holland tells what he calls a 'tragically prophetic' story about the young Wilde seeing the young Carson across a Trinity quadrangle and saying to a companion: 'There goes a man destined to reach the very top of affairs', to which the companion replied: 'Yes, and one who will not hesitate to trample on his friends in getting there.' However, this was written with the wisdom of several decades' hindsight, and is more than a little uncharitable towards Carson who, after all, declined to appear in the later trials once he realized that Oscar was to be in the dock rather than his client Lord Queensberry.

Frank Harris has, for once, no 'intimate details' of Wilde's life at Trinity, though he does have him remembering that other students there were 'worse even than the boys at Portora: they thought of nothing but cricket and football, running and jumping; and they varied these intellectual exercises with bouts of fighting and drinking. If they had any souls they diverted them with coarse "amours" among barmaids and the women of the streets; they were simply awful. Sexual vice is even coarser and more loathsome in Ireland than it is in England.'

Still, Oscar lasted his full three years at Trinity, even making a few friends, one of whom he is said to have invited home to meet his mother – 'she and I are founding a society for the suppression of virtue'. Nevertheless his own virtue seems to have been largely unassailed, and when his brother spoke to some fellow Trinity undergraduates in defence of prostitution (at a meeting chaired by no less a person than his father) Oscar is reported to have been thoroughly ashamed and embarrassed for both of them. It might thus be considered that when, in 1874, he not only passed out of Trinity with honours but also into Magdalen College, Oxford, with a demyship worth £95 a year, part of his delight lay in finally escaping from the shadow of his elder brother, who conspicuously failed to continue his academic career beyond Dublin.

Oscar was to go up to Magdalen in October, at the time of his twentieth birthday. Years later, he wrote that there had been two great turning points in his life: 'the first when my father sent me to Oxford, the second when Society sent me to prison'.

2
OXFORD

—

1874–1878

It requires a peculiarly innocent, closed or otherwise occupied mind to read Oscar Wilde's letters to and about his Oxford student contemporaries without reaching the conclusion that though he may have arrived there unversed in the ways of the flesh, he left Magdalen a thoroughly experienced homosexual, though not without romantic longings for members of the opposite sex. Otherwise, Oscar's Oxford life is a little hard to fathom: although it was by no means uncommon in the 1870s for Trinity College, Dublin, graduates to continue their education by reading for a second degree at either Oxford or Cambridge, there is nothing to indicate what Oscar himself thought he was doing there beyond escaping from a somewhat claustrophobic Irish life and a dominating mother back home in Dublin.

When he arrived at Magdalen, Oxford was still the university of Jowett and Spooner, and it seems that almost at once Oscar made himself a home there – a home which was to condition and shape his character over the next few years with almost astonishing speed and totality. The first of countless Wilde anecdotes are linked to Magdalen, though it is impossible a hundred years later to decide how many of them to believe. For Wilde, like Noël Coward a couple of generations later, achieved early in his twenties the reputation for being a 'wit'. As a result, most good off-the-cuff remarks made in Britain between about 1875 and 1895 were ascribed to him by one teller or another, on the principle that anecdotes improve if the key figure in them is recognizable.

Among that legion of Oxford anecdotes I am however inclined to believe that when reprimanded for leaving a certain history tutor's lectures at half-time, on the grounds that such behaviour was 'hardly the way to treat a gentleman', Oscar replied: 'But that tutor, Sir, is not a gentleman,' since snobbery of an ingrained Victorian kind was already a part of his character. I am less inclined to believe that he encountered the wrath of Canon Spooner by recounting Bible stories to

him as if he would never have come across them himself, though (like many but by
no means all of the pranks accredited to Oscar) it *is* a funny idea and could con-
ceivably have been his.

What we do know as unassailable fact about Oscar at Oxford is that his first two
years there were spent flirting with Rome and his last two flirting with Aestheticism,
though only the second flirtation really became a lasting engagement. The Roman
interest did not prevent him becoming a Freemason of the thirty-third degree
(Scottish Rite, Oxford University Chapter), but like many other post-Newman
Oxford students of his time he was sorely attracted by the more glamorous trappings of Catholicism – several visitors to Oscar's rooms in Magdalen noted that it
was 'filled with photographs of the Pope and Cardinal Manning'.

But Oscar's own letters are the best witness to his Oxford days. Written to a
select group of friends with nicknames like 'Kitten' (Reginald Harding), 'Bouncer'
(William Ward), and 'Julia' (Charles Harrison Tindal), they are masterpieces of
camp, gossipy writing in which sexes are transposed, and there are already nervous
inquiries about the limits of public tolerance – such as this, in a letter to William
Ward written in August 1876:

Last night I strolled into the theatre about ten o'clock and to my surprise saw Todd
and young Ward the quire [sic] boy in a private box together, Todd very much in the
background. He saw me so I went round to speak to him for a few minutes. He told me
that he and Foster Harter had been fishing in Donegal and that he was going to fish
South now. I wonder what young Ward is doing with him? Myself I believe Todd is
extremely moral and only mentally spoons the boy, but I think he is foolish to go about
with one, if he *is* bringing this boy about with him. You are the only one I would tell
about it, as you have a philosophical mind, but don't tell anyone about it like a good
boy – it would do neither us nor Todd any good. He looked awfully nervous and
uncomfortable. I thought of Mark.

But Oscar himself, known now as 'Hoskie' to his more intimate friends, had by
no means cut himself off from female society; vacations at Moytura were spent in
the company of Florence Balcombe, by all accounts a beautiful girl with whom
he was much taken, but who was later to become Mrs Bram Stoker, the wife of
Irving's general manager who was also the author of *Dracula*. There are stories of
'beauty parties' held in Wilde's Magdalen rooms at which elegant young ladies and
their chaperones took tea in surroundings not surely so very far different from
those he was to dramatize in his stage comedies two decades later.

Oxford also led him into more strenuous pursuits, such as starting to build a
road linking the nearby villages of North and South Hinksey, an abortive project
started by John Ruskin (then the university's Slade Professor of Fine Art) with a
view to teaching his students a little about the realities of life in general and
altruism in particular. Oscar himself recounted the road-building adventure to a

suitably impressed American audience during his lecture tour there eight years later:

One summer afternoon in Oxford we were coming down the High Street – a troop of young men going to river or tennis court or cricket field – when Ruskin, going up to lecture in cap and gown, met us. He seemed troubled, and prayed us to go back with him to his lecture, which a few of us did; and there he spoke to us, not on art this time, but on life, saying that it seemed to him to be wrong that all the best physique and strength of the young men in England should be spent aimlessly on cricket-ground or river, without any result at all except that if one rowed well one got a pewter pot, and if one made a good score a cane-handled bat. He thought, he said, that we should be working on something that would do good to other people, at something by which we might show that in all labour there was something noble. Well, we were a good deal moved, and said we would do anything he wished. So he went round Oxford and found two villages, Upper and Lower Hinksey, and between them there lay a great swamp, so that the villagers could not pass from one to the other without many miles of a round. And when we came back in winter, he asked us to help him to make a road across this morass for these village people to use. So out we went, day after day, and learned how to lay levels, and break stones, and wheel barrows along a plank – a very difficult thing to do. And Ruskin worked with us in the mist and rain and mud of an Oxford winter, and our friends and our enemies came out and mocked us from the bank. We did not mind it much then, and we did not mind it afterwards at all, but worked away for two months at our road. And what became of the road? Well, like a bad lecture it ended abruptly – in the middle of the swamp. Ruskin was going away to Venice, when we came back for the next term there was no leader, and the 'diggers' as they called us fell asunder. And I felt that if there was enough spirit amongst the young men to go out to such work as road-making for the sake of a noble ideal of life, I could from them create an artistic movement that might change, as it has changed, the face of England.

It says more than a little for Oscar's ability to get carried away by his own rhetoric that he apparently failed to notice that the road had in fact got no nearer to reality than his own 'artistic movement', and was to remain equally abortive. But these Oxford years, reading classics at Magdalen on a combined parental and college allowance of £200 annually, were happy ones for Oscar, arguably the first in which he found himself and knew what he wanted to be – which was, above all, famous. Wilde was not (as subsequent legend has had it) a flamboyant student; the early Oxford photographs show a soberly dressed, rather tweedy young man, apparently addicted to curly brimmed bowler hats; and although he was later to express his contempt for the Magdalen faculty ('One cannot live at Oxford because of the dons – in all else it is a most pleasant city') he achieved a first in Moderations and managed to come under the spell – often simultaneously – of the Pope, the Freemasons, Cardinal Manning, the Russian Nihilists (about whom he was to write his first play some years later), the European Socialists, Bulwer Lytton, Disraeli, George du Maurier and the Aesthetes. Oscar was nothing if not impressionable, and to each group he was able to give his individual and vociferous enthusiasm often for minutes at a time. He was talking at this period of 'the luxury of going over wholeheartedly to the Church of Rome', but admitted in letter after letter that his 'two greatest Gods' were Money and Ambition.

To achieve these, the first requisite was clearly to make himself noticed; but how? Oscar began, painstakingly, to create the image of an artist. 'Would that I could live up to my blue china' was one of his more studied remarks, and it is not hard to imagine his delight at finding it quoted in an Oxford chapel sermon as an example of the evil thoughts of modern undergraduates. Yet his attempts to convince heartier fellow-students that he was a poet and dreamer not of their ilk conflicted with his old Trinity enthusiasm for a fight. Frank Benson, the actor, who was up at Oxford with Wilde, recalled later an evening when:

Four intruders burst into the victim's room, the others following upstairs as spectators of the game. To the astonishment of the beholders, number one returned into their midst, propelled by a hefty boot-thrust down the stairs; the next received a punch in the wind that doubled him up on the top of his companions below, a third form was lifted bodily and hurled onto the heads of the spectators. Then came the triumphant Wilde, carrying the biggest of the gang, like a baby in his arms. He was about Wilde's size and weight, and hefty at that. But his struggles were useless and he was borne by Wilde to his own rooms and buried by Wilde underneath a pile of the would-be ragger's fine furniture.

Poet or pugilist, it doesn't much matter; Oscar's aim was attention and as he wasn't to get that through his writing for several years to come, it would have initially to be through his personality. His first poem was published during his second year at Oxford: called 'Chorus of Cloud Maidens' ('Cloud Maidens that float on for ever,/Dew-sprinkled, fleet bodies, and fair,/Let us rise from our Sire's loud river,/Great Ocean, and soar through the air'), it appeared in November 1875 in the Dublin University magazine for which both his parents had written in the past. Although Oscar did not think highly enough of it to include it in his first collected volume published six years later, one that did survive into this volume, written towards the end of Oscar's stay at Magdalen, commemorated the romanticism of his Oxford days:

Magdalen Walks

The little white clouds are racing over the sky,
And the fields are strewn with the gold of the flower of March,
The daffodil breaks under foot, and the tasselled larch
Sways and swings as the thrush goes hurrying by . . .

And the sense of my life is sweet! though I know that the end is nigh:
For the ruin and rain of winter will shortly come,
The lily will lose its gold, and the chestnut bloom
In billows of red and white on the grass will lie.

And even the light of the sun will fade at the last,
And the leaves will fall, and the birds will hasten away,
And I will be left in the snow of a flowerless day
To think on the glories of Spring, and the joys of a youth long past.

Yet be silent, my heart! do not count it a profitless thing
To have seen the splendour of sun, and of grass, and of flower!
To have lived and loved! for I hold that to love for an hour
Is better for man and for woman than cycles of blossoming Spring.

But despite the creeping shadow of Swinburne there, it was John Ruskin who most influenced Wilde during his time at Magdalen. In Oscar's first term the Ruskin lectures were entitled 'Aesthetic and Mathematic Schools of Florence', and in his first long vacation the following summer he made a pilgrimage in Ruskin's footsteps to Milan, Padua, Venice, Verona and Florence, wondering at the marvels of Italian architecture. With his travelling companion John Pentland Mahaffy (Oscar's old tutor from Trinity College, Dublin) he reached Milan on 22 June 1875, and from there wrote home to his mother of their travels:

Left Florence with much regret on Saturday night; passed through the Apennines, beautiful Alpine scenery; train runs on side of mountains half-way up; above us pine-forests and crags, below us the valley, villages and swollen rivers. Supper at Bologna; about 5.30 in the morning came near Venice. Immediately on leaving the mountains a broad flat tableland (there are no hills in Italy – mountains or flat plains) cultivated like a rich garden. Within four miles of Venice a complete change; a black bog, exactly like Bog of Allen only flatter; crossed over a big laguna on a bridge and arrived at Venice 7.30. Seized on immediately by gondoliers and embarked with our luggage into a black hearse-like barge, such as King Arthur was taken away in after the final battle. Finally through long narrow canals we arrived at our hotel, which was in the great Piazza San Marco – the only place in Venice except the Rialto anyone walks in . . . here we spent the morning; afterwards took a gondola and visited some of the islands off Venice; on one an Armenian monastery where Byron used to live. Went to another, the Lido, a favourite place on Sunday, and had oysters and shrimps. Returned home in the flood of a great sunset. Venice is a city just risen from the sea; a long line of crowded churches and palaces; everywhere white or gilded domes and tall campaniles; no opening in the whole city except at the Piazza San Marco. A great pink sunset with a long line of purple thunderclouds behind the city. After dinner went to the theatre and saw a good circus . . .

But unlimited European travel was not within the Wilde family budget for 1875, and by the end of June he was indignantly telling his mother in a letter that he had been forced by lack of funds to abandon Mahaffy in Milan and start for home by way of Paris. This first European journey was nonetheless to give Wilde some of his best poems (all of which, with the one notable exception of 'The Ballad of Reading Gaol', were to be written either while he was still up at Magdalen or within a year of going down in 1878), and by the time he returned to college for the Michaelmas term he was, at least in his own eyes, a poet.

In this year 1875–6 at Oxford, a second major influence was to be added to that of Ruskin. Walter Pater, then a don at Brasenose, was already the apostle of a new religion – novelty above all. He wrote:

While all melts under our feet we may well catch at any exquisite passion, or any contribution to knowledge that seems by a lifted horizon to set the spirit free for a moment, or any stirring of the senses, strange dyes, strange colours and curious odours, or the work of the artist's hands, or the face of one's friend . . . With this sense of the splendour of our experience and of its awful brevity, gathering all we are into one desperate effort to see and touch, we shall hardly have time to make theories about the things we see and touch. What we have to do is to be forever curiously testing new opinions and courting new impressions.

It was, to Oscar, an attractive new philosophy, since it forgave almost anything and he was already feeling an almost Catholic need for forgiveness of sins, whether real or imagined. By coincidence Pater, Dr Dodgson (Lewis Carroll) and Ruskin, all three writers and teachers with a distinct aversion to grown women, were together at Oxford in Oscar's undergraduate time, and it was of course Frank Harris who detected something distinctly queer about Pater's interest in Oscar. He has a graphic description of a private tutorial which ended with Pater falling to his knees and kissing Oscar's hands, a somewhat unlikely event, since Pater was so pathologically shy that he even taught in a whisper, allowing Oscar to remark that his lectures were not so much heard by his students as overheard.

Meanwhile Wilde's flirtation with the Catholic Church continued, and he was unwise enough to inform his family of it, thereby ensuring that when one particularly Protestant uncle died he left Willie Wilde a thousand pounds but Oscar a mere hundred, a legacy for which one suspects Oscar never wholly forgave the Church of Rome. More serious economic problems arose in the following April (1876), when Oscar's father died leaving seven thousand pounds but also a good many debts, which were to haunt Oscar and his mother for several years to come. That year, holidays were spent with an uncle in Lincolnshire rather than on the Continent, and belts were being tightened throughout the immediate family. Still, it was not an altogether unhappy time: a few months after Sir William's death, Oscar was writing to his friend Ward of his triumphant First in Mods:

My dear Boy, I know you will be glad to hear I have got my First all right. I came up from Lincolnshire to town on Monday and went down that night to Magdalen to read my Catullus, but while lying in bed on Tuesday morning with Swinburne (a copy of) was woke up by the Clerk of the Schools to know why I did not come up. I thought I was not in till Thursday. About one o'clock I nipped up and was ploughed immediately in Divinity and then got a delightful *viva voce*, first in the Odyssey, where we discussed epic poetry in general, dogs and women. Then in Aeschylus where we talked of Shakespeare, Walt Whitman and the *Poetics*. We had a long discussion about my essay on Poetry in the Aristotle paper and altogether [I] was delightful. Of course I knew I had got a First, so swaggered horribly . . . My father would have been so pleased about it. I think God has dealt very hardly with us. It has robbed me of any real pleasure in my First, and I have not sufficient faith in Providence to believe it is all for the best – I know it is not. I feel an awful dread of going home to our old house, with everything filled with memories . . .

Other letters written around this time indicate that Oscar was conscious of family sorrow, but in sadness as in triumph he was ever theatrical, and somehow his grief at parental loss seems to have had more to do with the way he thought readers of his letters would expect him to feel than the way he actually did.

That autumn Oscar started his third year at Oxford and fell in with Frank Miles, a man who was, in the view of Rupert Croft-Cooke: 'one of those sophisticated queers who tell women what they should wear, have rather exaggerated good manners and camp outrageously, preferably among titled people. He was frivolous and amusing and inherited from his mother some rather facile artistic gifts which he (at the time he met Wilde) was already devoting to pastel portraiture, chiefly of famous actresses.' By 1876 Miles had already left Oxford officially but was still lurking around the town, usually in the company of Lord Ronald Sutherland Gower. The theory is that Wilde found in Miles and his aristocratic friend not only homosexual allies but also a means of social advancement; Gower was after all a Lord at a time when being a Lord both mattered and forgave much. But it was Miles who was his real friend: they holidayed together at Moytura, the Wilde country house in County Mayo later described by Oscar as 'an absurd Irish property' but in fact a fishing retreat of considerable charm.

With Miles, Oscar began to invade London society as well as the Irish countryside; he also began to publish more of his poems, usually in the *Irish Monthly* or the Dublin University magazine – poems as often as not based on his earlier voyage to Italy:

> Italia! thou art fallen, though with sheen
> Of battle-spears thy clamorous armies stride
> From the north Alps to the Sicilian tide!
> Ay! fallen, though the nations hail thee Queen
> Because rich gold in every town is seen,

And on thy sapphire-lake in tossing pride
Of wind-filled vans thy myriad galleys ride
Beneath one flag of red and white and green.

Other poems written at this time included the 'Requiescat' for his dead sister and an appallingly sub-Wordsworthian 'To Milton':

Milton! I think thy spirit hath passed away
From these white cliffs and high-embattled towers;
This gorgeous fiery-coloured world of ours
Seems fallen into ashes dull and grey,
And the age changed unto a mimic play.

Then, in the third of Oscar's Easter vacations from Oxford, came another European tour. This time, again in the company of his first mentor Mahaffy (and two student friends, one of whom was George Macmillan of the publishing family), Oscar set off for Greece. An earlier plan had been that they should go first to Rome, where another friend called Hunter-Blair had promised to arrange an audience with the Pope, but Mahaffy insisted that they should make straight for Athens – in his view Wilde had already come too heavily under the influences of Pater's Aestheticism and Rome's Catholicism, and the sooner he could be brought back to a classical discipline the better. Nor did Mahaffy care about doing this reconversion gently: his own letters reveal that another of the party, William Goulding, had christened Oscar 'Snooks' on account of 'his swagger – which we shall knock out of him soon enough'.

By-passing Rome, the party reached Greece by way of Genoa and Ravenna, the latter a city which was to give Oscar the inspiration for his Newdigate-winning poem a year later. From Corfu, at the end of an exhaustive tour of Greek antiquity in the course of which he had nevertheless found time to get himself photographed in full-skirted Athenian costume, Oscar wrote an apologetic letter to his tutor at Magadalen:

My dear Mr Bramley, My old tutor Mr Mahaffy, Fellow of Trinity College Dublin, met me on my way to Rome and insisted on my going with him to Mykenae and Athens. The chance of seeing such great places – and in such good company – was too great for me and I find myself now in Corfu. I am afraid I will not be able to be back at the beginning of term. I hope you will not mind if I miss ten days at the beginning; seeing Greece is really a great education for anyone and will I think benefit me greatly, and Mr Mahaffy is such a clever man that it is quite as good as going to lectures to be in his society.

We came first to Genoa, which is a beautiful marble city of palaces over the sea, and then to Ravenna which is extremely interesting on account of the old Christian churches in it of enormous age and the magnificent mosaics of the fourth century. These mosaics were very remarkable as they contained two figures of the Madonna enthroned and receiving adoration; they completely upset the ordinary Protestant idea that the worship of the Virgin did not come in till late in the history of the Church.

I read the book you kindly lent me with much interest; the Roman Catholics certainly do seem to confuse together Catholic doctrines, which we may all hold, with the supremacy of the Pope which we need not hold.

I hope your health has been good this Easter. We expect to be in Athens by the 17th and I will post back to Oxford immediately.

In fact, Oscar did not 'post back to Oxford immediately'; instead he stopped off in Rome to join up at last with Hunter-Blair and have his long-postponed audience with the Pope. Years later, Hunter-Blair wrote:

I am sure that my companion remembered to his dying day the words of the venerable father as he placed hands of benediction on his head and expressed the hope that he would soon follow his condiscipulus into the City of God. Wilde spoke no word as we drove back to our hotel in our open carriage. Arrived there he locked himself in his room. When we met later he presented me with the MS of a poem which he had written with the impression of the visit to the Vatican still fresh in his soul:

> Oh! joy to see before I die
> The only God-anointed King

That April day was I think the high water mark of Oscar Wilde's rapprochement to the Catholic Church.

But all was not exactly sweetness and light when Oscar finally got back to Magdalen three weeks after the start of Trinity term. Mahaffy had already been severely reprimanded for his late return to Dublin, and Wilde was fined £45 and rusticated for the rest of the summer by the Magdalen authorities.

Oscar's fourth and final year at Oxford was however to be a considerable triumph: returning in the October of 1877 he worked hard and achieved another First in his finals the following summer, by which time he had also been awarded the prestigious Newdigate Prize for 'Ravenna', a poem Oscar read aloud (in his first solo public appearance) before the Chancellor at a ceremony in the Sheldonian:

> O how my heart with boyish passion burned,
> When far away across the sedge and mere
> I saw that Holy City rising clear,
> Crowned with her crown of towers! – On and on
> I galloped, racing with the setting sun,
> And ere the crimson after-glow was passed,
> I stood within Ravenna's walls at last!

Impressed by the double triumph of a First in Greats and the Newdigate (and their fury of the previous summer long forgotten), Magadalen offered to extend Wilde's demyship for another year, but Oscar had had enough of Oxford life, and felt the time had come for him to establish a wider reputation. 'Ravenna' was published by the University Press, thus becoming his first printed work in hard covers, and its success might have been expected to confirm his ambition to be a poet. By now, however, his intentions were both more complex and more vague; all Oscar knew for certain was that he had to move from the cloistered, academic world of Magdalen to the equally cloistered but more intriguing world of artistic London, where both his mother and his brother had already settled – Lady Wilde in the hope of conquering new salons, Willie in the hope of becoming a journalist.

But what of Oscar? Asked by his friend Hunter-Blair in the summer of 1878 what his real ambition was, he had replied: 'God knows; I won't be an Oxford don anyhow. I'll be a poet, a writer, a dramatist. Somehow or other I'll be famous, and if not famous, I'll be notorious. Or perhaps I'll lead the life of pleasure for a time and then – who knows? – rest and do nothing. What does Plato say is the highest end that man can attain here below? To sit down and contemplate the good. Perhaps that will be the end of me too.'

3
THE SELLING OF
OSCAR WILDE

—

1878–1881

Oscar arrived in London with (as he was later to inform a surprised American customs officer) nothing to declare except his genius, and even that was open to some doubt. His last Oxford year had been a stately progression through a series of applauding parties (at one of which, given by Mrs Morrell, he had dressed in all the finery of Prince Rupert), and by the time he reached London his greatest hope must have been that people would talk about him there as they had begun to within the narrower confines of Oxford ('There is only one thing worse in the world than being talked about and that is not being talked about').

Wilde had style but, at this time, little else; the money left by his father had been largely swallowed up by Dr Wilde's own debts, 'Ravenna' was not exactly proving to be a best-seller, and Oscar knew only that he wanted to be famous, not what he wanted to be famous for. He had grown his hair down towards his shoulders and with what little money was available to him (would it be wholly unjustified to guess that a certain amount of this came from those wealthier, more aristocratic young men whose intimate friendship Wilde had established at Magdalen?) he bought some velvet coats, soft silk shirts and long flowing ties. 'There goes that bloody fool Oscar Wilde,' a passer-by was once heard to remark. 'It is quite extraordinary,' Oscar said to whichever friend he was strolling through London with at the time, 'how quickly one becomes known.'

While other friends and contemporaries from Magdalen had gone on to more or less respectable careers in the army, the Church or the law, Oscar worked unceasingly on his own image – one which had to be created and sustained without the help of modern media. Long before the mechanical aids of radio or television or the cinema, years even before *Punch* began showing any interest in him, Wilde had to market himself virtually from door to door. The first thing he learned was that to be a celebrity in the London of the late 1870s it was necessary to associate with celebrities, and if he could not at first actually manage to associate with them he could at least address them. From Oxford he had already begun sending his poems to Mr Gladstone, and now that he was actually living in London he began writing odes and sonnets in praise of the leading figures of the day. Among his many greater achievements, it was Oscar who first began to use the phrase 'beautiful people' to describe those richer or more famous or better-connected than himself, and in that sizeable category he discovered a remarkable selection of talent.

The end of the severe mid-Victorian period had resulted in a positive outburst of London artistic energy, but it was not so much a movement (although Oscar would later try to dub it 'The Aesthetic Movement' in order to give himself something of which to be a leader) as a feeling in the air of Chelsea. Hesketh Pearson explains:

The poet, the painter, the architect, the sculptor, the dress-designer, the house-decorator, the furniture-maker, the printer; these had reacted against the stereotyped art and craft of the period, and their general tendency was called aesthetic, the work of each being in some way related to the rest, though the relationship was never clearly defined and few of the artists would have claimed kinship with others working along the same lines. Such diverse characters as Ruskin, Morris, Pater, Swinburne, Whistler, Woolner, Rossetti, Burne-Jones, Henry Irving, and even those satirists of the 'movement' Gilbert and Sullivan were part of the tendency; but it may be doubted if any of them would have cared to be called aesthetes, and the last two would have rejected the appellation with scorn. Each of these artists was playing his own game; and though some might have recognized that the others were on their side, none would have called it a team.

Oscar himself at this time, indeed at all times, was far from the poetic buffoon later illustrated by du Maurier and dramatized by Gilbert. The point about his behaviour was not that he did in fact walk down Piccadilly with a lily in his hand but that he made people believe it was the kind of thing he and he alone would do – in itself a far more satisfying achievement, since it established a reputation based on fantasy, one which could be trimmed and adapted and reconstructed to suit the prevailing winds of any given season.

Publicly, Oscar also began to acquire a number of suitable friends – often women highly placed in the society of the time (the Duchess of Westminster was one such), who found his attention and flattery a welcome change from the company of their hunting-shooting-fishing husbands. But privately there was still no doubt where Oscar's sexual affections lay: his first London address, an apartment at 13 Salisbury Street, off the Strand, he shared with Frank Miles, who had by then begun to make his name as an artist. Together, they battered on the doors of the famous.

They were careful however to keep their private life discreet, and Oscar was evidently aware that his reputation was not yet strong enough to withstand any hint of scandal. A poem he had originally written as 'Wasted Days', with an opening line reading: 'A fair slim boy not made for this world's pain', was revised before publication and turned into the more acceptable 'Madonna Mia', a tribute to Lily Langtry, now beginning: 'A lily-girl, not made for this world's pain'. 'After such terrible treacle,' sniffed one critic, 'well might Mrs Langtry cry "Save me from my friends".' But Oscar was keen to establish an 'interest' in girls – girls like Bernard Shaw's elder sister, for instance, a singer called Lucy Shaw, on whose account Shaw and Wilde met first in London at the salon Lady Wilde was trying to establish in Park Street, a house she had bought for herself and Willie with the proceeds from their sale of 1 Merrion Square.

Willie himself had begun to make a few friends in Fleet Street, and was thus able to introduce his younger brother to one or two editors who took individual poems of his, such as 'Athanasia' (published in *Time*) and 'Queen Henrietta Maria' (published in *Waifs & Strays*). Oscar had by now a sizeable backlog of unpublished poetry, mostly written as a result of his Oxford vacation travels, and finding its inspiration either in Greek antiquity, Italian architecture or first visits to the tombs of Keats and Shelley. Romantic to the point of schmalz, the poems were imitative, over-decorated and charming, which is probably much what one would have said of their author at this time.

One of the most remarkable aspects of Wilde's career at this point was that there was no solid achievement of any kind on which to build it. After all, it was not until 1888 that he was to publish *The Happy Prince*, with *The Picture of Dorian Gray* following two years later and the comedies all in the 1890s. Yet fully a decade earlier, in 1879, Wilde was already becoming well known. For what? For being around, for being in the right places at the right times with the right people, and for being unforgettable, or at any rate unmistakable, even across a crowded room.

Luck, immaculate timing and some valuable Oxford friendships all helped him on the road to fame (though not to fortune, which was to elude him throughout his short life). On 28 November 1879, he was writing to his friend Reginald Harding: 'I am going tonight with Ruskin to see Irving as Shylock and afterwards to the Millais ball. How odd it is. Dear Reg, ever yours, Oscar.' It seems likely, as Rupert Hart-Davis suggests, that on that first night of *The Merchant of Venice* at the Lyceum Wilde met Irving for the first time; within a month he had published a sonnet to Irving's partner Ellen Terry, who had played Portia at that performance:

> I marvel not Bassanio was so bold
> To peril all he had upon the lead,
> Or that proud Aragon bent low his head
> Or that Morocco's fiery heart grew cold:
> For in that gorgeous dress of beaten gold
> Which is more golden than the golden sun
> No woman Veronesé looked upon
> Was half so fair as thou whom I behold.

For her part Ellen thought Oscar one of the 'two most remarkable men I have ever met' (the other was Whistler), and recalled years later that when she set sail from Liverpool to tour America as Portia, Oscar was on the quayside sporting curly hair much after the fashion of the late Prince Regent – 'curly hair', noted a bystander, 'to match his curly teeth', thereby uncharitably drawing attention to the feature of which Oscar was least proud, since his teeth were also discoloured (in later life he would always cover his mouth with his hand when he laughed).

But Ellen was only one of four actresses whom Oscar openly courted in his first London years, one suspects as much for their publicity value as for their beauty. The first had been the Jersey Lily, Lily Langtry, favourite of the Prince of Wales (nothing but the best for Oscar), who had sat not only for Whistler and Burne-Jones but also for Wilde's friend Frank Miles, which was how they met soon after Oscar came down from Oxford. He published a sonnet 'to L.L.', calling her 'Helen formerly of Troy now of London' and then chose a particularly snowy night to sleep on her doorstep until he was booted out of the way by an indignant Mr Langtry on his way home from his club. Still, it was all good for the image, and when Mrs Langtry politely told Oscar to stop wasting his time with her, the 'foolish boy' rapidly turned his attention and his sonnets to Helen Modjeska, the distinguished Polish actress who was having a tremendous London success in the spring of 1880. For her Oscar did the 'rough translation' of one of her own native poems, an achievement all the more remarkable when you consider that Oscar spoke no Polish whatsoever. After Modjeska, who else but that other great European tragedienne Sarah Bernhardt, who somewhat to her surprise once stepped off the ferry at Folkestone to find Oscar shouting 'Vive Sarah' and flinging armfuls of lilies at her feet.

To ladies who proved more inaccessible, Oscar did not hesitate to write; in 1880 alone we find him scribbling fan letters to Geneviève Ward, Mrs Bancroft and the novelist Margaret Raine. Some idea of his rapidly improving social life can be gleaned from a letter written to Miss Ward in April or May of that year: 'I suppose you are very busy with your rehearsals. If you are not too busy to stop and drink tea with a great admirer of yours, please come on Friday at half-past five to 13 Salisbury Street. The two beauties – Lady Lonsdale and Mrs Langtry – and Mamma, and a few friends are coming . . .'

But by the August of 1880 a chronic shortage of money had forced Oscar and Frank Miles to move from Salisbury Street to cheaper rooms in Tite Street, Chelsea, where Oscar was to live most of his life from then until the disasters of 1895. Money was a constant problem, since neither Miles nor Oscar was getting much in return for their artistic labours. Their friendship, too, was becoming more than a little strained. Both had 'other interests', male and female, besides each other (Miles had a fancy for very young girls, notably the fifteen-year-old parlour maid in Salisbury Street), and they began to move apart as Wilde struggled onward and upward along the social ladder. Miles was eventually to die in an insane asylum in 1891.

Beyond writing sonnets to celebrated actresses. Oscar occupied himself with becoming the perfect all-purpose party guest. 'To get into the best society now-adays,' he was later to write, 'one has either to feed people, amuse people or shock people – that is all.' Oscar was too poor, though, often to do the first and still too cautious often to do the last. Instead he amused them, taking care to start with the ladies. 'No man has any real success in this world,' he also wrote, 'unless he has got women to back him, for women rule society.' Thus, at Grosvenor House and elsewhere, Oscar would be found in the very best company, discreetly relating gossip and raising polite titters with a well-rehearsed anecdote; a flamboyant dresser now (light trousers, flowered waistcoat, while silk cravat, lavender gloves), and a considerable charmer, he remained totally 'acceptable' in polite society.

Again, his great achievement during these months was not actually to be outrageous (which would merely have limited his social horizons) but to seem outrageous, and it is said that even the heartiest of sporting clubmen, those most likely to deride him and despise his preciosity, were swiftly won over by his manner. Oscar was above all else a very funny man, drawing for his humour not only on a good basic knowledge of the late Victorian trendies but also on the discovery that by simply replacing a single word in a sentence with the most unlikely word to be found in that context ('If one tells the truth one is sure sooner or later to be found out') he could regularly raise a laugh . . . laughter which was to re-echo through the four high-society comedies he wrote ten years later.

Wilde's conversational technique was impeccable: rather than try to dominate a dinner party from the outset, he would start talking very quietly to his neighbour, making sure he could be heard by at least one other person, until all around him had fallen silent. Not that everyone was delighted with him: Augustus Hare, deploring the ways of the modern generation, wrote in his journal:

Mrs M.L. had recently met this type of an aesthetic age staying at a country house and described him going out shooting in a black velvet suit with salmon-coloured stockings and falling down when his gun went off, yet captivating all the ladies by his pleasant talk. One day he came down looking very pale. 'I am afraid you are ill, Mr Wilde,' said one of the party. 'No, not ill, only tired,' he answered, 'the fact is, I picked a primrose in the wood yesterday and it was so ill, I have been sitting up with it all night.'

Others were more enthusiastic. Laura Troubridge, for instance, the cousin of one of Oscar's Magdalen contemporaries, wrote in her own journal: 'July 1879; to the National Gallery, saw Sarah Bernhardt there, had a good stare at her, met Tardy and went together to tea at Oscar Wilde's – great fun, lots of vague intense men, such duffers, who amused us awfully. The room was a mass of white lilies, photographs of Mrs Langtry, peacock feather screens and coloured pots, pictures of various merit.'

Socially, Oscar had thus achieved within his first year in London all he could possibly have hoped; celebrated guests were invited to sign their names on the white panels of his Chelsea apartments, and had there been fully-fledged gossip columns or television chat shows in 1879 Oscar would doubtless have been forever in them, occupying gradually more and more space. The problem was, however, that being a celebrity or even a celebrity-seeker was not of itself financially promising. Most of his new-found friends had already established reputations for acting or writing or painting: Oscar, though he constantly acted (as himself) and wrote almost daily, was still not getting any real money for it – and the more he socialized, the more money he seemed to need.

Big brother Willie, now a journalist on a literary paper called *The World*, was doing his best to introduce Oscar to editors who might be forthcoming with commissions, but there was as yet very little to show. Such poems as Oscar had published in the smaller literary magazines relied for their celebrity mainly on the people to whom they were addressed, and most of his letters to editors in 1880 began 'Mr Oscar Wilde begs to enclose for the approval of the Editor . . .' – approval which was all too seldom granted. True, Clement Scott had accepted his translation of the Modjeska poem for *Routledge's Christmas Annual*, and there were a few guineas here and there for individual sonnets, but it was not anything like enough to keep Oscar in the style to which he was rapidly becoming accustomed. Nor had the move from the Strand to Chelsea saved much, and with Frank Miles beginning to attract police attention for his curious sexual habits (one night Oscar had to lean against the street door while Frank made his escape from an inquisitive constable over the rooftops) Wilde had begun to feel more and more strongly that it was time to get his own career onto a stable, reliable foundation from which it could not be shaken by the occasional indiscretion or an embarrassing lack of funds.

Poetry alone was evidently not going to provide any solution, but during 1880 Oscar had formed a close albeit quiet friendship with Johnston Forbes-Robertson's younger brother Norman. Encouraged by this, and by his already expressed if more platonic devotion to Bernhardt and Modjeska, Wilde began to think more and more in terms of the theatre. A playwright stood, after all, to make considerably more money than a poet, always assuming he could come up with a successful play, and the whole atmosphere of the stage appealed to Oscar more strongly than the colder world of publishing. Early in 1880 he had begun to work on *Vera, or The Nihilists*, a drama of unique inadequacy, full of lines like 'She is a dangerous woman, then, this Vera Sabouroff?' which suggest nevertheless another possibility; had Oscar been born half a century later he would almost certainly have ended up in Hollywood writing costume dramas for Louis B. Mayer.

'*Vera*', as its alternative title suggested, was about nihilism in Russia, but its message was a romantic one. 'The modern Nihilistic Russia,' wrote Oscar, 'with all the terror of its tyranny and the marvel of its martyrdoms is merely the fiery and fervent background in front of which the persons of my dream live and love.' It requires little imagination to suppose that *Vera* was rapidly shown to Modjeska and Bernhardt, perhaps even to Lily Langtry for good measure. The first person to express any real interest in it was however Mrs Bernard Beere, who, inspired by the assassination of Tsar Alexander II in March 1881 (an event which linked British and Russian politics more closely, since the new Czarina was to be the sister of the Princess of Wales), announced that she would be producing the play in the following December with herself in the title role.

It never happened: three weeks before the first performance an announcement to the Press stated: 'Considering the present state of political feeling in England, Mr Oscar Wilde has decided on postponing for a time the production of his drama *Vera.*' The rumour was that the Prince of Wales had personally intervened to stop the production of a 'pro-revolutionary' play at this difficult time, but it seems equally possible that Mrs Beere had simply re-read the script and had understandable second thoughts. Even so, there are faint traces of the Wildean style which was to reach such expert maturity ten years later:

PRINCE PAUL: To make a good salad is to be a brilliant diplomatist – the problem is entirely the same in both cases. To know exactly how much oil one must put with one's vinegar.

BARON RAFF: A cook and a diplomatist! An excellent parallel. If I had a son who was a fool I'd make him one or the other.

PRINCE PAUL: I see your father did not hold the same opinion, Baron . . . For myself, the only immortality I desire is to invent a good sauce.

And although Oscar's playwriting career may have started somewhat shakily, he had at least achieved his primary aim – an escape from total obscurity. In February 1880 George du Maurier had begun his celebrated series of *Punch* caricatures of the aesthete, usually named 'Maudle' or 'Jellaby Postlethwaite'; these caricatures displayed an insufferably precious young man propped against a mantelpiece or leaning languidly on an umbrella, while uttering superior witticisms. They were originally intended as a satire of the Bohemian world in general and Swinburne in particular. As the months passed, however, the character in du Maurier's drawings came to look more and more like Wilde – or was it that Wilde took care to look more and more like the caricature?

Either way, by the end of 1881 there was little doubt in the public mind that Oscar Wilde was the man being satirized by *Punch*, a misapprehension which neither *Punch* nor Wilde strove officiously to correct. When therefore in that same year the then editor of *Punch*, F. C. Burnand, wrote a play called *The Colonel*, in which there was a swindling, charlatan dandy called Lambert Streyke, there was again the feeling that this was intended as a parody of Wilde, though it could again have been a more generalized attack on 'the aesthete'. Beerbohm Tree played the role, and also appeared as 'Scott Ramsey', yet another stage impersonation supposedly of Wilde, in two subsequent plays, *Where's The Cat?* and *The Charlatan*.

The only difficulty in seeing Wilde as the all-purpose dandy poet of the kind satirized by *Punch* was that unlike Swinburne he had not actually published much, apart from 'Ravenna' after it won the Newdigate – and that volume appears not to have found many London readers. In 1881 however Oscar obligingly rectified this omission by publishing at his own expense a collection called simply *Poems*, into which he threw virtually all his other Oxford work together with the Greek poems and all the sonnets to and about actresses. The volume attracted rave reviews from *The World* (where Willie Wilde was by now reviewing poetry) but a sharply hostile attack from *Punch* itself, which called the poems 'Swinburne and water' and added 'the poetry's Wilde but his poems are tame'.

Oscar, undaunted, sent copies to Robert Browning and Matthew Arnold and the long-suffering Mr Gladstone among other celebrities, most of whom replied with politely non-committal thanks. *Punch* apart, the most damning criticism of Oscar's first collected works came not from a critic but from a member of the Oxford Union which Oscar had joined but seldom been active in during his four years at Magdalen. When the Union's librarian announced that Mr Wilde had presented a copy of his *Poems* to the society, Oliver Elton rose to object:

It is not that these poems are thin – and they are thin; it is not that they are immoral – and they are immoral; it is not that they are this or that – and they are all this and all that; it is that they are for the most part not by their putative father at all, but by a number of better-known and more deservedly reputed authors. They are in fact by William Shakespeare, by Philip Sidney, by John Donne, by Lord Byron, by William Morris, by Algernon Swinburne, and by sixty more, whose works have furnished the list of passages which I hold in my hand at this moment. The Union Library already contains better and fuller editions of all these poets; the volume which we are offered is theirs, not Mr Wilde's; and I move that it be not accepted.

The book was returned by the Union to its author, and Oscar's mood was not improved by the glee with which *Punch* reported, also in that autumn of 1881, the cancellation of his play: 'The production of Mr Oscar Wilde's play *Vera* is deferred. Naturally no one would expect a veerer to be at all certain; it must be like a pretendedly infallible forecast, so weather-cocky. *Vera* is about Nihilism; this looks as if there were nothing in it.'

All in all, Wilde's prospects by the end of 1881 must have been considered somewhat dim; he had lost the sheen of a newly-arrived social sensation, he was now too familiar a sight around London drawing rooms to be considered out-rageous any more, and his initial attempts at poetry and playwriting had been little short of disastrous.

Oscar was saved, as later he was to be ruined, almost accidentally; in the April of 1881, when the vogue for satirizing 'the aesthete' had been at its height, Richard D'Oyly Carte had presented a new comic opera by Gilbert and Sullivan called *Patience*. In it was a character called Bunthorne, important enough to have his name in the opera's subtitle, 'Bunthorne's Bride'. Modelled partly on Rossetti, partly on Swinburne, and perhaps fractionally on Wilde, Bunthorne is the 'perfectly precious' young aesthete who in the story eventually loses the girl he loves for being, in a word, too camp. The opera was a considerable success when it opened at the Opéra Comique in the Aldwych; the critic of a weekly called *The Era* noted: 'I gazed with furtive curiosity on my neighbours, and confess that the presence of so many representatives of the Good, the Beautiful and the True filled me with surpassing awe . . . a fierce clamour of screams, yells and hisses which descended from the Gallery signalled the arrival of Mr Oscar Wilde himself . . . there, with the sacred daffodil, stood the exponent of uncut hair, Ajax-like, defying the Gods.'

D'Oyly Carte subsequently decided that *Patience* was strong enough to survive an Atlantic crossing, and made plans for its American presentation under the auspices of Colonel W. F. Morse, an astute American manager and publicist whose view it was that the show would go down rather better in America if someone could alert its audiences to the existence of the 'aesthetes' in advance. Otherwise, he wrote to Carte, the whole production would be liable to fall rather flat, since very few Americans had the remotest idea what an aesthete actually was, let alone why Gilbert and Sullivan should have gone to the trouble of creating an entire opera to mock one.

Accordingly, Morse cabled Oscar in Tite Street asking if he would consider a personal-appearance tour, making fifty speeches across the length and breadth of America in advance of the touring *Patience* company. Oscar's reply was immediate: 'Yes, if offer good.' The deal was that he would get all his expenses plus one-third of the box-office takings in each of the towns he and *Patience* played, and after the exchange of a series of letters Oscar set sail aboard the *Arizona* for the New World on Christmas Eve 1881. What, after all, had he to lose? London theatres were scarcely clamouring for his plays, publishers did not appear all that keen on more poetry (his first collection had gone into four editions, but they were small ones), and he had little money with which to keep up the all-important appearances of the time. In America, there was always the chance that he might make some real money, or at the very least find a management willing to produce *Vera*.

Punch bade Oscar a not wholly charitable farewell. Beneath the drawing of a sorrowful lady waving adieu to the *Arizona*, a caption read: 'Design by our own Greenery-Yallery-Grosvenor-Gallery Young Man, in humble imitation of the picture by Professor W. B. Richmond, symbolizing "The Grief of Aestheticism at the Departure of Her Oscar".'

4
COAST TO COAST: AMERICA

—

1882

America brought out the best and the worst in Wilde: for the first (and perhaps last) time in his life he was being paid to do the one thing he really enjoyed, which was to be himself only more so. He was following in the footsteps of Charles Dickens (a considerably more familiar name in America when he began his readings there in 1867), and trail-blazing for Dylan Thomas and Brendan Behan in that line of distinguished British authors who have barnstormed their way across America in search of money, alcohol, fame, or combinations of all three.

And, mercifully for Oscar, America was to supply him with a whole new series of targets – starting with the Atlantic ocean he had to cross to get there. 'It was disappointing,' he told reporters who met him on his arrival in New York on 2 January 1882; though on his return to England a year later (presumably a rougher crossing) he added, 'The Atlantic has been greatly misunderstood.' It was on this first arrival in New York that Wilde was able to inform a customs officer that he had nothing to declare except his genius, and within a day or two he was also able to announce that: 'In America, life is one long expectoration.' He was also much troubled by the speed of American life ('Everybody seems in a hurry to catch a train. This is a state of things which is not favourable to poetry or romance') and by its lack of pageantry ('There are no trappings, no pageants, no gorgeous ceremonies. I have seen only two processions: one was the Fire Brigade preceded by the Police; the other was the Police preceded by the Fire Brigade').

For its part America viewed Oscar with a mixture of delight and despair, having seen nothing quite like him. At his opening speech in New York, a week after he landed and some months after the première of *Patience* there, he was able to remind his audience: 'You have listened to the charming music of Mr Sullivan and the clever satire of Mr Gilbert for 3 hundred nights and I am sure having given so much time to satire it is not asking too much to ask you to listen to the truth for one evening.'

Having thus set the mood for what was to come, Oscar embarked on a solo turn rather than a speech – one created out of a mixture of instruction, comment and gossip, including quotations from Ruskin and Pater as well as his own earlier witticisms. The official title for the lecture was 'The English Renaissance', and Oscar obligingly dressed for the occasion in Bunthorne garb, complete with knee-breeches. There had however been a couple of ugly encounters with Colonel Morse at which Oscar had refused to be seen anywhere except on the podium in such clothes, and had also refused to be seen carrying sunflowers or any kind of flowers down Broadway. Though the Colonel was providing the means for Oscar's American travels, Oscar was already astute enough to realize that he had to sell himself to America as Oscar Wilde, not as an off-stage personification of Bunthorne.

The morning after his début at the Chickering Hall, New York, on 9 January 1882, a writer in *The Nation* observed: 'Mr Wilde is essentially a foreign product and can hardly succeed in this country. What he has to say is not new, and his extravagance is not extravagant enough to amuse the average audience. His knee-breeches and long hair are good as far as they go; but Bunthorne has really spoiled the public for Wilde.' The critic of the *New York Tribune* was, however, rather less dismissive:

The most striking thing about the poet's appearance is his height, which is several inches over six feet, and the next thing to attract attention is his hair, which is of a dark brown colour, and falls down upon his shoulders . . . The complexion, instead of being the rosy hue so common in Englishmen, is so utterly devoid of colour that it can only be said to resemble putty. His eyes are blue, or a light grey, and instead of being 'dreamy' as some of his admirers have imagined them to be, they are bright and quick – not at all like those of one given to perpetual musing on the ineffably beautiful and true. Instead of having a small delicate hand, only fit to caress a lily, his fingers are long and when doubled up would form a fist that would hit a hard knock, should an occasion arise for the owner to descend to that kind of argument . . . One of the peculiarities of his speech is that he accents almost at regular intervals without regard to the sense, perhaps as a result of an effort to be rhythmic in conversation as well as in verse.

As Wilde's lecture tour proceeded, and as the success of his appearances established him more and more firmly in his own (rather than Gilbert and Sullivan's) right, Oscar abandoned any references to Bunthorne, a state of affairs which the Colonel intensely disliked but could do little about, since the original terms of their contract had referred only somewhat vaguely to 'lectures' in the town where *Patience* was due to play, rather than to any specific ticket-touting.

In the twelve months which followed his initial appearances in New York, Oscar lectured all over North America to audiences which included Oliver Wendell Holmes, Louisa May Alcott, General Grant, Walt Whitman and Longfellow, most of whom confided to their diaries that they found him 'amazing', 'extraordinary' or just plain 'strange'. The Press sent him up sky high, making veiled references to the homosexuality of which he was even in America already suspected, and there might have been an ugly occurrence in Boston had it not been for Oscar's ever-ready wit. A large number of Harvard students turned up for his lecture there, all carrying sunflowers and all set to barrack him. 'I see about me,' said Oscar quickly, 'signs of an already established American Aesthetic Movement. As I look about me I am impelled for the first time to breathe a fervent prayer: God save me from my disciples.' The local paper subsequently reported: 'Everyone who witnessed the scene on Tuesday evening must feel about it much as we do, and those who came to scoff, if they did not exactly remain to pray, at least left the Music Hall with feelings of cordial liking and, perhaps to their own surprise, of respect for Oscar Wilde.'

Oscar's letters, written during this year to such faithful English friends as Norman Forbes-Robertson and Mrs Bernard Beere, bear witness to the extent of his travels across America between his arrival in January and his return to New York in September. Their datelines include Philadelphia, Washington, Niagara Falls, Chicago, Cincinnati, St Louis, Bloomington, Griggsville, St Paul, Omaha, Sioux City, San Francisco, Salt Lake City, Kansas City, Topeka and Columbus, Ohio, to say nothing of Montreal, Toronto and ultimately Augusta, Georgia. Nor were his travels altogether without incident: though delighted with his New York success ('The hall had an audience larger and more wonderful than ever Dickens had'), Oscar was soon involved in a bitter quarrel with Archibald Forbes, a British war correspondent currently also on the American lecture trail. It had been agreed that Wilde would go to one of Forbes's Baltimore lectures, but the two men had little in common and a great deal to differ about (Forbes, according to Rupert Hart-Davis, lectured with his medals on and had no time for Oscar's brand of dress reform). On the train from Philadelphia to Baltimore they quarrelled. Oscar refused to alight at the station and travelled on to Washington, thereby missing Forbes's lecture and infuriating local residents as well as Forbes himself. Soon afterwards Wilde was writing to an ailing D'Oyly Carte back in England, demanding a decent road manager and warning: 'Another such fiasco as the Baltimore business and I think I would stop lecturing.'

By Chicago (12 February) his temper had improved, however, and he was writing of his success to Mrs George Lewis:

For lecturing in Chicago I received before I stepped on the platform a fee of 1,000 dollars – £200 for one hour's work – that is answer enough [to the English Press, which was suggesting that Oscar's American tour had turned into something of a disaster]. Of course in smaller places I get less, but never less than £40 ... I have a sort of triumphal progress, live like a young sybarite, travel like a young god ... I am deluged with poems and flowers at every town, have a secretary writing autographs all day, and would be bald in half a week if I sent the locks of hair I am asked for through the post every morning.

Despite all this adulation, Oscar found time in the early stages of his tour to revise the luckless *Vera*, and D'Oyly Carte obligingly made arrangements to have it published in America while Wilde was there. By the end of March he had reached San Francisco, from where he wrote to Forbes-Robertson:

There were 4,000 people waiting at the 'depot' to see me, open carriage, four horses, an audience at my lecture of the most cultivated people in 'Frisco, charming folk. I lecture here again tonight, also twice next week; as you see I am really appreciated by the cultured classes. The railway have offered me a special train and private car to go down the coast to Los Angeles, a sort of Naples here, and I am feted and entertained to my heart's content. I lecture here in California for three weeks, then to Kansas; after that I am not decided. These wretched lying telegrams [reports that Wilde was still failing on the lecture circuit] in the *Daily News* are sent by Archibald Forbes, who has been a fiasco in his lecturing this season and is jealous of me. He is a coward and a fool. No telegram can kill or mar a man with anything in him. The women here are beautiful.

But in San Francisco Wilde was subjected to an ordeal by drink (one he overcame, predictably, by drinking all those present under the table), and earlier, in Colorado, he had found himself in even rougher territory:

While I was lecturing at Denver, I received a message that if I went on to Leadville as I proposed to do, the harsher spirits there would be sure to shoot me or my travelling manager. I wrote and told them that nothing they could possibly do to my travelling manager would intimidate me . . . and I went. My audience was mainly composed of miners whose huge sombre hats, red shirts and high boots made me think of seventeenth-century cavaliers. Indeed they were the first really well-dressed men I had seen since my arrival in the United States . . . They sat there, rows and rows of them, enormous, powerfully built men, silent as the grave, their eyes watchful, their brawny arms folded over their muscular chests, a loaded gun on each thigh . . . I spoke to these delightful fellows of the early Florentine Schools, and they slept as peacefully as though no crime had ever stained the ravines of their wild mountain home. I described to them the pictures of Botticelli: the very name, that seemed to them, I daresay, like some newly-invented American drink, roused them from their dreams. I read them passages from the autobiography of Benvenuto Cellini, and he proved so popular that they asked as one man 'Why had I not brought him with me?' I explained that Benvenuto had been dead for some years, which elicited the demand 'Who shot him?'

They afterwards took me to a dancing saloon, where I saw the only rational method of art criticism I have ever come across. Over the piano was printed a notice: 'Please do not shoot the pianist – he is doing his best.' The mortality among pianists in that place is marvellous. Then they asked me to supper, and having accepted I had to descend a mine in a rickety bucket in which it was impossible to be graceful . . . I opened a new vein, or lode, with a silver drill, the lode being named 'The Oscar'. I had hoped that in their grand simple way they would have offered me shares in 'The Oscar', but in their artless untutored fashion they did not.

From there it was on into the Deep South, where Oscar noted a deep melancholy, attributable, he decided, to the recent Civil War: 'How beautiful the moon is tonight,' I remarked once to a gentleman standing near me; "Yes," was his reply, "but you should have seen it before the war." '

Wilde then travelled north again to Canada, pausing only to look at the Niagara Falls ('Every American bride is taken there, and the sight of this stupendous waterfall must be one of the earliest, if not one of the keenest, disappointments of American married life') before going on to lecture in each of the major Canadian towns. By now he had reached the end of his first contract with Morse, and was able to renegotiate for expenses plus sixty per cent of the gross, with a minimum guarantee of two hundred dollars every time he stepped up to the rostrum.

But most of the big American towns had already been played by both Oscar and *Patience*, and Wilde was fast tiring of the smaller ones. 'Will you lecture us on aesthetics?' the mayor of Griggsville had wired. 'Yes,' replied Oscar, 'if first you'll change the name of your town.' On reflection, though, this tour of America had already proved all he could have expected and more. 'Let me gather its golden fruits,' he had written to a new acquaintance, the actor-playwright Dion Boucicault 'that I may spend a winter in Italy and a summer in Greece amidst beautiful things,' and the gold had by now safely reached the pockets of the huge fur coat he had acquired in Canada and in which he was to be photographed for almost ever afterwards.

On his travels, Oscar had met ex-slaves, brothel keepers and confidence tricksters; he had been introduced into a New World and introduced as a celebrity, and the assurance he acquired across the States was only to depart from him in a courtroom thirteen summers later. In one town he had seen them auctioning a doorknocker which had but recently belonged to Jesse James, and on his way to others he had seen canyons and prairies and mountains and lakes on a scale which had left even Oscar temporarily speechless.

Yet through it all, through a few failures and a great many successes (the latter achieved in the teeth of Press hostility, since journalists were always among the last to be won over by Oscar's heavyweight charms), he never lost sight of the basic self-knowledge which America had brought him. At twenty-six Wilde had discovered that his bisexuality could not be totally suppressed, but he had also discovered that it afforded a basis on which to build a public character – one who might initially irritate and even infuriate his audiences, but who also knew how from that unpromisingly hostile beginning to win them over to affection and even admiration before the evening was out. Oscar's promoters in America had expected him to do no more than pave the way for Bunthorne; instead he offered a totally different stage character, one of infinitely more interest and complexity, and having precious little to do with Gilbert and/or Sullivan.

His private life on tour seems to have been erratic: there is a curious account of him 'running Wilde' after some boys in Toronto, and another odd incident involving a poet called James Rennell Rodd, with whom he had been on a walking tour of France in the previous year. While in America Oscar arranged to have some of Rodd's verses published there; unfortunately however he also persuaded the publishers to delete Rodd's original dedication to his father and to insert instead 'To Oscar Wilde, Heart's Brother, These few Songs and many Songs to come', a substitution which did not delight Mr Rodd nor, presumably, his father. It was the end of yet another beautiful friendship.

In all, Oscar gave about seventy-five lectures in America between January and July, but he never lost sight of his other reason for being there – his search for a producer for *Vera*. By the middle of July he was back in New York, where he stayed (except for a brief outing to Halifax, Nova Scotia, and a return engagement to speak in Boston) until the middle of December. When, in October, Mrs Langtry arrived from England, Oscar was on the pier to greet her with the inevitable lilies. 'I would rather,' he told some surprised bystanders, 'have discovered Mrs Langtry than have discovered America.' In that ecstatic mood he reviewed her Broadway début in *An Unequal Match*, writing a notice for the *New York Herald* which tactfully detailed her beauty but not her acting, which by all other newspaper accounts left on that occasion a good deal to be desired.

An American actress called Marie Prescott had by now expressed some interest in *Vera*, though Oscar was unhelpful when she began asking for some minor alterations – 'Who am I,' he snapped, 'to tamper with a masterpiece?' In the event, *Vera* was not staged in New York until the August of 1883, and then only for a week, but in the meantime Oscar had started work on a new verse drama called *The Duchess of Padua* which he hoped another celebrated American leading lady of the time, Mary Anderson, would produce and star in. By now, however, he was fast learning the economics of Broadway, and before leaving New York he confirmed the deal. 'I accept your terms' (he wrote in November to Miss Anderson's stepfather and manager, Hamilton Griffin) 'for writing a play for Miss Anderson. Will you have an agreement drawn up with the agreed-on terms: $1000 down: $4000 when it is finished: the play to be ready by March 31st and played before a year from now . . . in surrendering the customary author's royalty I have been actuated by a wish not to allow a money matter to stand in the way of an artistic success.' Either by that, or by an astute realization that five thousand 1882 dollars in the hand would be rather better than a percentage of an as yet unfinished play which might or might well not draw in the Broadway crowds.

Oscar left America on 27 December 1882, bound for Liverpool on the *Bothnia*. It is not clear quite how much of his American profits he had managed to save, though the last three months of good living in New York had probably accounted for a fair part of them. Looking back on his time there he was able to remember, and inevitably to exaggerate, his successes. He had written to Forbes-Robertson at one stage of the tour:

I have two secretaries, one to write my autograph and answer the hundreds of letters that come begging for it. The other, whose hair is brown, to send locks of his own hair to the young ladies who write asking for mine; he is rapidly becoming bald. Also a black servant, who is my slave – in a free country one cannot live without a slave – rather like a Christy Minstrel, except that he knows no riddles. Also a carriage and a black tiger who is like a little monkey. I give sittings to artists, and generally behave as I have always behaved – dreadfully.

But he was able also to account for every moment of a year well spent exploring both America and his own potential for drawing crowds. From New York harbour he fired one parting shot:

'When good Americans die they go to Paris; when bad Americans die they stay in America.'

5

LONDON, PARIS
AND BACK TO NEW YORK

—

1883–1884

Oscar returned to London, but not for long: the thousand-dollar advance from Mary Anderson and Hamilton Griffin was still intact, and with it he decided that the time had come to conquer Paris, home of the artists he had so long admired (and who surely could be persuaded in their turn to admire him?), and obviously the best place to work on *The Duchess of Padua*. By the end of January 1883 he was thus installed in rooms at the Hôtel Voltaire on the left bank of the Seine; it was here that Oscar first met the poet and journalist Robert Harborough Sherard, great-grandson of William Wordsworth, and the man who was to be Wilde's most faithful and frequent biographer in later years, as well as his most constant if irritating ally.

Arriving to collect Oscar from the Voltaire one morning, Sherard happened to admire the view from his bedroom window across the Seine to the Louvre. 'That,' replied Oscar, 'is altogether immaterial, except to the proprietor who of course charges it with the bill. A gentleman never looks out of the window.' But the Oscar whom Sherard first met that winter was no longer quite the same man who had barnstormed America so recently. Instead, Wilde was in more humble mood – in Paris to work and to worship at the shrines or at least the salons of such of his heroes as Edmond de Goncourt, Alphonse Daudet, Victor Hugo, Emile Zola, Verlaine, Mallarmé and Henri de Régnier. Chief among his idols at this time, however, was the novelist Honoré de Balzac, as Sherard later reported:

In the daytime, when he was at work, Oscar dressed in a white dressing-gown fashioned after the monkish cowl that Balzac used to wear at his writing table. At that time he was modelling himself on Balzac. Beside the dressing-gown, he had acquired an ivory cane with a head of turquoises, which was a replica of the famous walking-stick which Honoré de Balzac used to carry when love had transformed the recluse into a fop. But he was not borrowing from the master these foibles of toilette alone. I think that at that time he was striving in earnest to school himself into labour and production. He was sated with social success, and had fixed a high ambition to carve out for himself a great place in English letters. He had inspired himself with that passage in *La Cousine Bette* in which Balzac declares that constant labour is the law of art as it is the law of life, and points to the fact that all great artists have been unresting workers.

It says a good deal for Sherard's fervent if platonic devotion to Oscar that he failed to see him even in these moods as a founder tenant of pseuds' corner ('a man who behaves like Balzac,' wrote St John Ervine later, 'should first take care to be Balzac'). Alas, however, Balzac's influence did not help Wilde to take Paris by storm, and the three months he spent there were peculiarly disastrous in terms both of work and of social contact. By the simple device of sending his collected poems to all and sundry, Oscar had collected enough invitations to cover virtually all the salons of the still small Parisian literary and artistic world. But each of his long-desired meetings with the famous went somehow awry: de Goncourt noted in his *Journal* only that he had met 'an individual of doubtful sex who talks like a third-rate actor', and Victor Hugo actually fell asleep during their first conversation. Nor were the Daudet family any more impressed with Wilde. Léon later recalled: 'His voice was at once pallid and fat, the words came tumbling out of his frightfully slack mouth, and when he had finished he would roar with laughter like a fat, satisfied, gossipy woman.'

So much for Oscar's dreams of taking Paris by storm. His stay there was ultimately remarkable for nothing more than the completion of *The Duchess of Padua* and the decision to abandon his still shoulder-length hair in favour of a more closely-curled, shorter cut which he had first admired on a bust of Nero in the Louvre, and which he insisted on taking a bemused barber to see and copy on him.

On 15 March, he sent the final script of *The Duchess of Padua* to Mary Anderson as promised. She responded rapidly but unenthusiastically ('the play in its present form, I fear, would no more please the public of today than would *Venice Preserved* or *Lucretia Borgia*'), and it was evident that Oscar would be getting no more money than he had already had from her. Sherard recalls his apparent indifference at receiving the bad news: 'Wilde opened [the telegram] and read the disappointing news without giving the slightest sign of chagrin or annoyance. He tore a tiny strip off the blue form, rolled it up into a pellet, and put it into his mouth. Then he passed the cable over to me, and said "Robert, this is very tedious." After that he never referred again to his disappointment.' He did however tell Sherard that they would have to be more economical in their choice of restaurants henceforward, since: 'We can no longer dine with "The Duchess".'

Many years later Oscar was to admit to Robbie Ross that the play was the only one of his works unfit for publication. It was however ultimately produced in New York at the Broadway Theatre in January 1891, but without Oscar's name

and under the new title *Guido Ferranti*. It did no better then than on its only other
sustained outing, a German production in Hamburg in 1904 during the run of
which one of the leading actors went out of his mind and had to be taken to an
asylum.

Lacking any such excitement, the script itself is concerned with the Duchess,
her lover Guido, and an intricate revenge plot of mind-bending complexity and
simultaneous banality, derived in roughly equal measure from echoes of John
Webster and William Shakespeare. The ever-loyal Sherard (in some ways the
forerunner of Alfred Douglas in Wilde's life, albeit sexually uninvolved and convinced almost until the bitter end that his old friend was innocent of such sordid
charges as those made in court) thought it 'a great play', but then anything Oscar
did was all right by him, including the payment of unexplained sums of money to
sailors who passed in the Paris night, an action memorably described by Sherard
as an example of Oscar's 'philanthropy'.

Staying in Paris until the last of the American money ran out, Oscar began to
reconsider his image yet again. After all, he had now tried his luck in the three
major capitals of the Western world and in each of them been considered at most
'diverting': pleasant certainly, witty perhaps, but an essentially frivolous being
who could be relied upon for the entertainment of an evening but little more, and
whose charms had a habit of wearing thin on repeated encounters. It was not
enough, Wilde realized, on which to base a career, nor had he yet discovered any
real alternative. The plays and the poems still showed signs of being dutifully
rather than enthusiastically written, and he had yet to find a poetic or theatrical
form into which he could channel his eccentric talent for rearranging well-known
phrases into one-line gags. He had begun to realize, moreover, that to be a social
butterfly was hardly man's work either, and he began somewhat nervously to
consider where he now should stand. 'The Oscar of the first period is dead,' he told
Sherard in Paris; 'we are now concerned with the Oscar of the second period.' But
what, precisely, was to be the difference, beyond a shorter haircut?

Searching around for new masters, Oscar lighted upon Charles Baudelaire,
whose theories of beauty-in-evil (*Les Fleurs du Mal*) were to become one of the
greatest influences on this second-period Wilde. In fervent imitation Oscar too
began absinthe-drinking, but although his intellect may have been striving
towards Baudelaire his heart was still very much in the theatre. Twice he was to be
found in the dressing-room of Sarah Bernhardt, warmly greeted as a long-lost
friend from London, still expressing extravagant adoration, and still perhaps
half-hoping for a script commission. None came; instead Oscar contented himself
with a minor feud with Emile Zola who, introducing Wilde at a literary dinner,
had concluded: '*Malheureusement M. Wilde sera obligé de répondre dans sa langue
barbare.*' Leaping to his feet, Oscar replied: '*Je suis Irlandais de naissance, Anglais
de race et, comme le dit M. Zola, condamné à parler la langue de Shakespeare.*'

Undeterred by his failure with *The Duchess of Padua*, Oscar spent the last few weeks of his Paris stay at work on 'The Sphinx', the first of his long poems to hint at secret vice. 'My first idea was to print only three copies,' he wrote of it later, 'one for myself, one for the British Museum and one for heaven. Then I began to have some doubts about the British Museum . . . as a poem it will doubtless destroy domesticity in Britain.' He also began to work on 'The Harlot's House', another perfervid ballad perched precariously on the borderline between vice and virtue.

But with no prospective buyers in sight the American advance was fast running out. By the beginning of May 1883 we find Oscar reluctantly refusing an invitation to visit a friend of Lady Wilde's in Rome, in all probability because he lacked the fare:

At present I am deep in literary work, and cannot stir from my little rooms over the Seine until I have finished two plays. This sounds ambitious, but we live in an age of inordinate personal ambition and I am determined that the world shall understand me, so I will now, along with my art work, devote to the drama a great deal of my time. The drama seems to me to be the meeting place of art and life . . .

A week or two later he was back in London, by now so totally broke that the first thing he did on returning home was to pawn the Berkeley Gold Medal he had won at Oxford. Soon he was writing to Sherard in Paris:

The splendid whirl and swirl of life in London sweeps me from my Sphinx. I am hard at work being idle; late midnights and famished morrows follow one another. I wish I was back in Paris, where I did such good work. However, society must be amazed, and my Neronian coiffure has amazed it. Nobody recognizes me, and everybody tells me I look young; that is delightful, of course.

Oscar's immediate prospects were, however much he tried to hide it from Sherard in the desperate gaiety of his letters, more than a little bleak. What ultimately saved his fortunes yet again was an offer to lecture on his American travels and also on 'The House Beautiful', the latter a 'fashion' speech which he was to give frequently over the next few years whenever an invitation and twenty-five pounds were offered. It was his American lecture, however, given in July 1883, which attracted the attention of *The Illustrated Sporting and Dramatic News*:

Yes, you can sound the trumpets and beat the drum (the big one). Our Oscar has returned. America has parted with the precious loan we made her, and Oscar is in dear happy England once again . . . Ah! how I counted the days and the hours until the time should arrive for the apostle of the true and the beautiful to meander on to the platform and deliver himself of his luxurious platitudes. At last it came. But why should I rack my soul with the memory of my great disappointment! O, America! What have you been and gone and done? This was not the long-haired and attentuated aesthetic we sent you. These are not the knee breeches we swathed him in when we set him afloat on the disappointing Atlantic . . . in short you have fattened our Oscar, you

have cut his hair, and you have returned him (this side up, with care) in a suit of very
ordinary dress clothes and a last-year's 'masher collar' . . . Postlethwaite is on the wane
and our own Oscar is about as gone a coon as you ever sent up a gum tree . . .

Alongside this review (bylined 'Our Captious Critic') there appeared four joky
caricatures of Oscar 'before and after' his American journey. The fourth of these,
by a chilling coincidence, showed him in convict's dress above the forecast that
prison was where Wilde would eventually find himself.

By the time of the America speech, Wilde had established an uneasy friendship
with the artist James McNeill Whistler, immortalized in any account of Oscar's
life as the man who actually said: 'You will, Oscar, you will' when Wilde at one
of their many subsequent Café Royal dinners expressed the wish to have personally
uttered some particularly good line. Whistler took a rather dim view of the way
in which almost all Oscar's thoughts on Art as expressed in his lectures turned out
to be watered-down and highly commercialized versions of his own. Nonetheless, in
their own eccentric ways, the two men had a lot in common; when, in the autumn
of 1883 *Punch* parodied one of their conversations about Sarah Bernhardt, Wilde
cabled to Whistler: 'Punch too ridiculous. When you and I are together we never
talk about anything but ourselves.' Whistler cabled back: 'No, no, Oscar, you
forget. When you and I are together we never talk about anything except me.'
But it was Wilde who had the last word: 'It is true, Jimmy, we talk about you, but
I think of myself.'

Yet Wilde's social life, even in his beloved Chelsea, was still not all that it might
be. Early in July he was forced to write to John Everett Millais: 'I am anxious to
have the privilege of being present at your Academy soirée, and not having had
the honour of receiving an invitation would esteem it a great kindness if you could
give me a card for it. I know how many calls there must be on you of the same kind,
so if I am too late in my request pray accept my excuses for troubling you.'

Money was still very tight, and Oscar had temporarily taken rooms in Charles
(later Carlos) Street off Grosvenor Square, then kept by a retired butler and his
wife 'for single gentlemen of distinction'. There was still very little work around for
Oscar, though he did have the promise, in the autumn, of a British lecture tour
again under the auspices of the redoubtable agent Colonel Morse, now resident in
England, who promised several bookings but 'no more than £25 a night'.

Encouraged by the prospect of future wealth, Oscar set sail in August from
Liverpool bound for New York, where Marie Prescott was at last about to stage
and star in his *Vera or The Nihilists* on Broadway. The first night, 20 August, at the
Union Square Theatre, was unpromising. Oscar did receive 'an ovation' (his own
description) after the second act, but there were alas two more acts to follow, and
by the end of the fourth, audience and critical opinion was sharply divided. The
New York Mirror reckoned *Vera* 'the noblest contribution to literature the stage

has received in many years', but the *New York Times* thought it 'unreal, long-winded and wearisome', and the latter was the prevailing view.

Vera folded after only a week in New York, though the fearless Miss Prescott insisted that if Oscar himself would take over the male lead opposite her they could recoup some of the money on tour and even perhaps make a small profit for themselves. Oscar, ever an actor, must have been sorely tempted, but he was contracted to his own autumn tour of English lecture halls, and reluctantly had to refuse. In September he set sail again from New York, this time never to return. *Punch*, ever gleeful when reporting news of fresh Wildean disasters, noted smugly that *Vera* must have been 'vera vera bad'.

6

CONSTANCE...
AND MARRIED LIFE

—

1884–1888

Back in London at the close of 1883, Oscar found himself and his career (which were by now largely one and the same) somewhat becalmed. The forthcoming provincial lecture tour (on which he was to alternate 'The House Beautiful' with 'Impressions of America') was all very well in its way, but it relied on a limited knowledge of the USA and an even more limited knowledge of interior decoration (the latter augmented by a few quotations from Whistler and other friends in the art world), and even Oscar realized that such credentials could not be made to last indefinitely. The essential difficulty here was one which was to persist throughout the 1880s, right up to the publication of *The Happy Prince* and *Dorian Gray* as the decade ended. Who precisely did Oscar Wilde think he was?

The question was to be asked – and vulgarly answered – in subsequent and more scandalous years, but for the moment it was purely an artistic one, and was asked mainly of Oscar by himself. Early intentions of becoming a poet had vanished with the early editions of his first published anthology – one which still owed rather too much of its form and content to Milton, Wordsworth and an assortment of other poets whom Oscar had read, remembered and copied – while any thoughts he had of being a playwright disappeared for the time being with the Broadway collapse of *Vera*.

So there he was, an itinerant lecturer in search as always of money and celebrity in roughly equal measure, but at this particular time in still more urgent need of some kind of artistic base from which to operate. In the London social and literary circles within which he continued to move, or at any rate to drift, and even in the circles where they paid good money to hear him speak, it was really not enough to be known simply as Oscar Wilde the well-known celebrity, especially as his friends and contemporaries from Oxford were all now beginning to carve out distinctive careers.

Oscar had nothing to offer, or indeed to live off, but himself, his memories of America and his ambitions, and the time was fast approaching when they would scarcely be enough to support him. Moreover the public's fascination with 'Aestheticism' was fading, and the mockery of *Punch* and Gilbert and Sullivan had lost its initial impetus, so that Oscar suddenly found himself in severe danger of being shifted from the foreground of avant-garde fashion to the background of a stale joke. His lectures were reasonably well-attended still, and they were enthusiastically received, but to a man whose career had thus far depended on being the shock-boy of a new world of artistic adventure, polite applause was really not enough. It was Oscar, still attuned to the demands of his audience, who was the first to realize that he would have to try something new. Even his earliest fans were beginning to go off him somewhat sharply, as this extract from Laura Troubridge's diary for July 1883 indicates:

Went to a tea party at Cressie's to meet the great Oscar Wilde. He is grown enormously fat with a huge face and tight curls all over his head – not at all the aesthetic he used to look. He was very amusing and talked cleverly, but it was monologue and not conversation. He is vulgar, I think, and lolls about in, I suppose, poetic attitudes with crumpled shirt cuffs turned back over his coat sleeves.

But throughout the autumn and winter of 1883–4, Oscar continued to tout himself around the country, returning to London in between 'dates' to keep in touch with such now well-established friends as Whistler and to make newer acquaintances – among them that of Frank Harris, who later recalled:

He shook hands in a limp way I disliked; his hands were flabby, greasy; his skin looked bilious and dirty. He wore a great green scarab ring on one finger. He was overdressed rather than well-dressed; his clothes fitted him too tightly; he was too stout. He had a trick which I noticed even then, which grew on him later, of pulling his jowl with his right hand as he spoke, and his jowl was already fat and pouchy. His appearance filled me with distaste. I lay stress on this physical repulsion, because I think most people felt it, and in itself it is a tribute to the fascination of the man that he should have overcome the first impression so completely and so quickly. I don't remember what we talked about, but I noticed almost immediately that his grey eyes were finely expressive; in turn vivacious, laughing, sympathetic, always beautiful. The carven mouth, too, with its heavy, chiselled, purple-tinged lips, had a certain attraction and significance in spite of a black front tooth which shocked one when he laughed ... he looked like a Roman Emperor of the decadence ... in ten minutes I confessed to myself that I liked him, and his talk was immensely quickening. He had something unexpected to say on almost every subject. His mind was agile and powerful and he took a delight in using it ... even when he merely reproduced what the great writers had said perfectly, he added a new colouring.

But charm and a good memory were scarcely enough to support Oscar in the style which his image already demanded, and it was therefore more than a little fortunate that, while lecturing in Dublin during the last week of November 1883, he once again met Constance Mary Lloyd, the daughter of a distinguished Irish barrister from Cork (Horace Lloyd, QC) who had died in 1874. Constance, upon the remarriage of her mother, had gone to live with her grandparents who made her the heiress to their small but respectable fortune. In 1881, when she was just twenty-four, she had first encountered Oscar at one of Lady Wilde's salons. 'He came yesterday' (she had written to her brother Otho) 'at about 5.30 and stayed for half an hour, begged me to come and see his mother again soon, which little request I need hardly say I have kept to myself. I can't help liking him, because when he's talking to me he's never a bit affected, and speaks naturally, excepting that he uses better language than most people.'

Two years later they met again. Oscar was booked to lecture on 'The House Beautiful' at the Gaiety Theatre, Dublin, and Constance again wrote to her brother: 'It occurred to our brilliant minds that perhaps O.W. would be in town that evening, so we left a note at the Shelbourne asking him to come in, and he accordingly did, and though decidedly extra affected, I suppose partly from nervousness, he made himself very pleasant . . . [we] were so delighted with the lecture that some of us intend going to 2/- places today' (to hear Oscar's American lecture, which he usually gave the day after 'The House Beautiful').

Constance even liked *Vera or The Nihilists* ('I really think it very fine. Oscar says he wrote it to show that an abstract idea such as liberty could have quite as much power and be made quite as fine as the passion of love – or something of that sort') and by 26 November, just three days after meeting Oscar again in Dublin, she was telling brother Otho to prepare himself 'for an astounding piece of news! I am engaged to Oscar Wilde and perfectly and insanely happy! I am sure you will be glad because you like him, and I want you now to do what has hitherto been my part for you, and make it all right. Grandpapa will, I know, be nice, as he is always so pleased to see Oscar. The only one I am afraid of is Aunt Emily . . .'

The family were in fact almost surprisingly agreeable to the marriage of Constance and Oscar. Even her aged grandfather, now known to be dying, rallied for a while at the news of their engagement, and although Frank Harris did not much care for Constance ('a young lady without any particular qualities of beauty') the general feeling in London and Dublin was that they were ideally suited to each other. Constance came of good though not irreproachable stock (her father had once been charged with indecently exposing himself to nursemaids in Hyde Park, a piece of irrelevant but intriguing background detail for which we have as usual to thank the diligent researches of Frank Harris), and she would be able to give Oscar the kind of home and resting place which until now had eluded him in adult life. More important still, she had a private income which was ideal in that it was not so great as to stop Oscar working, nor yet so little as to leave him perpetually touring the nation in search of a few pounds for a lecture.

Oscar, of course, saw the whole affair more romantically than that. 'I am going to be married,' he wrote to his old flame Lily Langtry, 'to a beautiful girl called Constance Lloyd, a grave, slight, violet-eyed little Artemis, with great coils of heavy brown hair which makes her flower-like head droop like a blossom, and wonderful ivory hands which draw music from the piano so sweet that the birds stop singing to listen to her . . .'

But the lecture tour could not be abandoned because of Oscar's new-found happiness, and he pressed on to Birkenhead, where he made a disciple of Richard Gallienne (later le Gallienne), whose father noted at the end of one of Oscar's more flamboyant lectures: 'The man is no fool.' On from there to Edinburgh, where Oscar met up again with his old Oxford travelling companion David Hunter Blair, by now a Catholic priest. But Oscar did not go well up north: his theories on the beautifying of industrial areas, involving as these did the removal of all workshops and factory chimneys to some remote island in the Channel and the return of Manchester to a community of simple shepherds, predictably failed to win him many new fans. It was therefore with something akin to relief that he returned to London and to safer territory. 'Do you like music, Mr Wilde?' he was asked after a recital at a private house. 'No,' replied Oscar, 'but I liked that very much.'

Music and art were, as ever, the two great touchstones for his one-liners. 'I like Wagner so much better than other composers,' was one such, 'because he is so loud that one can talk the whole time without the risk of being overheard.' And faced, at the Royal Academy Summer Exhibition, with Frith's famous *Derby Day*, Wilde merely inquired: 'And he did all that by hand?'

The friendship between Wilde and Whistler was now at its height, and there began those lengthy Café Royal repasts which were to be a regular feature of Oscar's diary for the next ten years. After lunch, as often as not, they would move on to the salon of Lady Wilde who was now living, still with Willie, in Park Street. But now there was Constance, and during their engagement 'my own darling Oscar' was nothing if not attentive. His letters indicate that he speeded back to Dublin between lectures to be close to her, and inside a white leather-bound copy of his 1881 collection of poems he wrote:

> I can write no stately proem
> As a prelude to my lay;
> From a poet to a poem
> I would dare to say.
>
> For if of these fallen petals
> One to you seem fair,
> Love will waft it till it settles
> On your hair.

And when wind and winter harden
All the loveless land,
It will whisper of the garden,
You will understand.

To Waldo Story, an American sculptor, Oscar wrote:

Her name is Constance and she is quite . . . quite perfect except that she does not think Jimmy [Whistler] the only painter that ever really existed; she would like to bring Titian or somebody in by the back door: however she knows I am the greatest poet, so in literature she is all right; and I have explained to her that you are the greatest sculptor; art instruction cannot go further. We are, of course, desperately in love. I have been obliged to be away nearly all the time since our engagement, civilizing the provinces by my remarkable lectures, but we telegraph to each other twice a day, and the telegraph clerks have become quite romantic in consequence. I hand in my messages, however, very sternly, and try to look as if 'love' was a cryptogram for 'buy Grand Trunks' and 'darling' a cypher for 'sell out at par'. I am sure it succeeds.

The marriage was on 29 May 1884, at St James's Church in Paddington, just around the corner from the house at 100 Lancaster Gate where Constance had lived when in London. By this time her grandfather was so ill that the wedding was supposed to be private, though a large crowd in fact gathered on the pavement to wonder at the dress of the bridal party. Oscar had taken special charge of this, and though conservatively dressed himself had ensured that the ceremony should be visually unforgettable. All the bridesmaids were in shades of yellow and wore dresses cut on the lines of Oscar's beloved classical Greek antiquity. The bride herself wore a high Medici collar, and one lady, almost certainly Lady Wilde, was to be found in a 'very aesthetic costume' of rich red silk with a hat of white lace trimmed with clusters of real roses.

Jimmy Whistler rather let the side down by sending a telegram which read: 'Fear I may not reach you in time for ceremony. Don't wait.' To which Oscar replied that they would not. 'Nor,' he added, 'will we be waiting for the dear Queen. In this fine weather I asked her to remain at Osborne.'

In the church register Oscar signed himself 'gentleman' and added that he was twenty-eight, either out of absent-mindedness or, more probably, because twenty-nine was already beginning to seem to him a little old. The reception was held at 100 Lancaster Gate, and the happy couple then set off for Paris, where the honeymoon was to be spent at the Hôtel Wagram on the Rue de Rivoli. There, somewhat surprisingly, they were joined at once by Oscar's faithful Parisian friend Robert Sherard. He called early on the morning after their arrival and, despite such curious timing, was warmly received by Oscar, who took him out for a walk while Constance was dressing. Passing through the Marché St Honoré, Oscar stopped to send a bunch of flowers back to the bride whom he had just left, a gesture which impressed Sherard as much as Oscar doubtless intended it should.

As the honeymoon progressed, however, Wilde spent an increasing amount of time with Sherard, who later recalled: 'He visited with me the haunts of the lowest criminals and poorest outcasts of the city, the show-places of the Paris Inferno – Père Lunette's and the Château Rouge – which everybody who wishes to know the depths of darkness which exist in the City of Light goes to see.' Whether Oscar was in 'the depths' purely as a curious tourist or in search of young men is not entirely clear from Sherard's account. It seems possible that with his marriage he had decided to start a new lease of life and suppress the homosexuality of his earlier years, but equally possible that he did not regard marriage as having very much to do with it one way or the other. He was, as he kept reminding Constance, an Artist, and an Artist must surely be allowed to be free from the everyday constraints of lesser folk.

Homosexuality, moreover, was hardly a subject to bring up in polite conversation with a lady of good background, even if the lady did happen to be your wife, and for her part Constance, like any good Victorian bride, was not about to question her husband's whereabouts at all times of the day or night even on their honeymoon. The chances are, I suspect, that Oscar now decided to leave his innermost sexual inclinations to take care of themselves, certain in the knowledge that they could be controlled and that what Constance didn't know couldn't hurt her.

Returning to London, the happy couple were suddenly faced with some of the less divinely romatic aspects of married life. Constance's fortune was considerably smaller than Oscar might have hoped, and a good deal of the ready money was going into the home they were having decorated at No. 16 (now 34) Tite Street by two old but not unextravagant friends, Jimmy Whistler and the architect and stage designer E. W. Godwin, who had lived for several years with Oscar's beloved Ellen Terry.

While the house was being made fit for an Artist to live in (Oscar, having lectured for so many months now on 'The House Beautiful', had to be supremely careful about the one where he himself would be seen to live), Mr and Mrs Wilde stayed first at the Brunswick Hotel, then when that proved too expensive with relations, and finally at Oscar's old bachelor lodgings in Carlos Street, where they remained until the Tite Street house was ready for them in December.

It was, after all, no ordinary Chelsea house. The combined labours of Whistler, Godwin, countless builders (one of whom Oscar took to court for inefficiency) and the happy couple themselves finally produced a dining room in shades of white and blue and yellow, a study complete with Moorish casements and bead curtains, and a drawing-room with white peacock feathers let into the ceiling. Almost midway through the renovation of what had been a rather ordinary Victorian terraced house, both Oscar and Constance began to worry, understandably, about their financial situation. Oscar went back hastily to his lecturing and Constance began to think somewhat frantically of ways to improve their joint income ('I am thinking of becoming correspondent to some paper, or else of going on the stage ... I want to make some money; perhaps a novel would be better. At present I am deep in *Les Misérables* which is wonderful'). She however was regarded as a mixed blessing by some of Oscar's older friends and acquaintances. Newspaper gossip columns referred to her as 'the Chatelaine of the House Beautiful', but the beady Laura Troubridge was less impressed: 'July 1884. Mr and Mrs Oscar Wilde to tea. She dressed for the part in limp white muslin with *no* bustle, saffron coloured silk swathed about her shoulders, a huge cartwheel Gainsborough hat, white and bright yellow stockings and shoes – she looks too hopeless and we thought her shy and dull. He was amusing of course.'

Oscar, meanwhile, was picking up the work where he could, and that summer was glad to take over from his brother Willie as drama critic on *Vanity Fair* when Willie went off for a short holiday in France. Then it was back to the lecturing, interrupted only by his court case against the builders at Tite Street, with whom he had inevitably quarrelled, though whether or not because of his insistence on the peacock feathers being let into the ceiling is not clear. By now he had added two new lectures to his repertoire ('Dress' and 'The Value of Art in Modern Life'), and with them he continued to travel the land throughout the autumn and winter of 1884–5.

By now he was very much the family man. Constance was pregnant (the first of their two sons, Cyril, was to be born in June 1885), and Oscar seems to have been content to hack his way around Fleet Street and the provinces, writing and lecturing on the arts. 'An intoxication with words' was one diagnosis of Oscar's condition at this time, but it paid some of the bills and enabled him to start regular reviewing for the *Dramatic Review* and *Pall Mall Gazette*. For the latter publication he once divided all books into three classes:

1. Books to be read, such as Cicero's *Letters*, Suetonius, Vasari's *Lives of the Painters*, the *Autobiography of Benvenuto Cellini*, Sir John Mandeville, Marco Polo, St Simon's *Memoirs*, Mommsen, and (till we get a better one) Grote's *History of Greece*.

2. Books to be re-read, such as Plato and Keats: in the sphere of poetry, the masters not the minstrels; in the sphere of philosophy, the seers not the *savants*.

3. Books not to be read at all, such as Thomson's *Seasons*, Rogers's *Italy*, Paley's *Evidences*, all the Fathers except St Augustine, all John Stuart Mill except the essay on *Liberty*, all Voltaire's plays without any exception, Butler's *Analogy*, Grant's *Aristotle*, Hume's *England*, Lewes's *History of Philosophy*, all argumentative books and all books that try to prove anything. This third class is by far the most important. To tell people what to read is, as a rule, either useless or harmful; for, the appreciation of literature is a question of temperament not of teaching; to Parnassus there is no primer and

nothing that one can learn is ever worth learning. But to tell people what not to read is a very different matter, and I venture to recommend it as a mission to the University Extension Scheme.

The late 1880s were not years of much distinction for Oscar, but they were those in which he learned the disciplines of journalism and a kind of concision which had eluded him in the past, but which was to serve more than well for his playwriting in the 1890s.

Vyvyan (later Vyvyan Holland), the second of the two sons Oscar and Constance were to have, was born in 1886 within fifteen months of Cyril (who was to die in the First World War), and the early years of Oscar's married life were thus heavily domestic, with Constance almost permanently pregnant. But marriage at first seems to have suited Oscar admirably, and his attitude to Constance was loving if somewhat patronizing, as though in her he saw the 'delightful child in need of care and protection' that so many Victorian husbands then saw in the women they married. There are no indications that Oscar looked elsewhere for friendship, at least until the time of Vyvyan's birth about three years into the marriage, when a Cambridge undergraduate called Harry Marillier appears somewhat shadily on the scene. All the same (as Hesketh Pearson has noted), Oscar's one-line jokes about marriage, if assembled in the order in which they were first written, do display an increasing lack of sympathy with the whole institution:

'The proper basis for marriage is a mutual misunderstanding.'

'The worst of having a romance is that it leaves one so unromantic.'

'The only difference between a caprice and a lifelong passion is that the caprice lasts a little longer.'

'Faithfulness is to the emotional life what consistency is to the life of the intellect – simply a confession of failure.'

'Women never know when the curtain has fallen. They always want a sixth act, and as soon as the interest of the play is entirely over, they propose to continue it.'

'In married life three is company and two is none.'

'One should always be in love. That is the reason one should never marry.'

'A man can be happy with any woman, as long as he does not marry her.'

'When one is in love, one always begins by deceiving oneself, and one always ends by deceiving others. That is what the world calls a romance.'

'The happiness of a married man depends on the people he has not married.'

'When a man has once loved a woman, he will do anything for her, except continue to love her.'

But for the time being all was well with the Chatelaine of the House Beautiful and her husband in Tite Street. Oscar seems to have found Constance something of an asset, a doll to be dressed up and shown off to friends at afternoon parties referred to as Constance's 'jours'. (At one of these however Oscar was heard to murmur: 'How beautiful Constance is – if only I could be jealous of her', which seems somehow less than reassuring as a compliment.) Richard le Gallienne also reports on Oscar at home, gently mocking Constance's religious fervour ('Missionaries, my dear? Surely you realize that missionaries are the divinely provided food for destitute and underfed cannibals? Whenever they are on the brink of starvation, Heaven in its infinite mercy sends them a nice plump missionary'), but all other contemporary accounts suggest blissful happiness interrupted only by the ever-present financial worries. Constance actually had to borrow from the neighbours during the early years of their marriage, while Oscar dodged tradesmen and tax collectors in order to continue an elaborate series of receptions for which the likes of Arthur Balfour, Sarah Bernhardt, Mark Twain, Lily Langtry, John Ruskin and Herbert Beerbohm Tree all came to Tite Street.

But this state of affairs clearly could not last forever. Early in 1885 Oscar had been appointed a regular book critic for the *Pall Mall Gazette*, but that was scarcely going to keep the wolf from the door of Number 16, and by the middle of July, within a month of Cyril's birth, we find him writing to his old Oxford contemporary George Curzon (later Viceroy of India and Foreign Secretary and already a man with some influence in the Conservative Party):

Dear Curzon, I want to be one of Her Majesty's Inspectors of Schools! This is ambition – however I want it, and want it very much, and I hope you will help me. Edward Stanhope has the giving away, and as a contemporary of mine at Oxford you could give me great help by writing him a letter to say (if you think it) that I am a man of some brains. I won't trouble you with the reasons which make me ask for this post – but I want it and could do the work, I fancy, well. If you could give me and get me any help you can I will be so much obliged to you, and I know how the party think of you – you brilliant young Coningsby! I hope to get this and to get it with your approval and your good word. I don't know Stanhope personally and am afraid he may take the popular idea of me as a real idler. Would you tell him it is not so?

Curzon obliged, but Oscar's ambitions in that direction were not realized and a regular job of any kind eluded him for another twelve months, by which time Vyvyan was on the way and the Wilde family fortunes had reached a dangerously low ebb. By now Constance was forced by her pregnancy to remain very much in the background, no longer the graceful ornament Oscar needed around Tite Street, and he himself had started writing fervently indiscreet letters to Marillier at Cambridge:

Harry, why did you let me catch my train? I would have liked to have gone to the National Gallery with you, and looked at Velasquez's pale evil King, at Titian's Bacchus with the velvet panthers, and at that strange heaven of Angelico's where everyone seems made of gold and purple and fire, and which for all that looks to me ascetic – everyone dead and decorative! . . . When am I to see you again? Write me a long letter to Tite Street, and I will get it when I come back. I wish you were here,

Harry. But in the vacation you must often come and see me, and we will talk of the poets ... I have never learned anything except from people younger than myself, and you are infinitely young.

For a brief interlude Oscar returned to poetry, recording in a sonnet his re-actions to the sale in 1885 of Keats' love letters ('These are the letters which Endymion wrote/To one he loved in secret, and apart/And now the brawlers of the auction mart/Bargain and bid for each poor blotted note'), reactions which sadly foreshadowed by just ten years the fate that was to befall many of his own manuscripts in more terrible times.

For now, however, Oscar was still highly pleased with himself ('I wish I could grave my sonnets on an ivory table') and continued to eke out a living from the lectures, the *Pall Mall Gazette* and the *Dramatic Review*, for which latter paper he covered the opening production at the New Theatre Oxford in February 1886 – an OUDS *Twelfth Night*, with Arthur Bourchier as Feste. He did however continue to urge his friends, including the formidable Mahaffy, to support him in his applica-tion to become an Inspector of Schools, a job Matthew Arnold had once held but for which Oscar seems to have been both educationally and sexually hugely un-qualified, even by his own bizarre standards of suitability. The job was never to be his, but luckily his need for it ended in the early spring of 1887.

Oscar, by now the father of two small boys, had spent another whole year in the uncertain pursuit of a reputation, a pursuit which had led him through still more lectures and reviews to the writing of his first really successful prose piece, a light-hearted transatlantic tale called 'The Canterville Ghost', which first appeared in print in the *Court and Society Review* for February 1887 before being reprinted a few weeks later in the *New York Tribune*. A mixture of social satire, burlesque and romantic sentiment, it was mainly remarkable for being the first in a series of widely varied prose pieces (among them 'The Model Millionaire', 'The Sphinx Without A Secret', and 'Lord Arthur Savile's Crime') which were to appear throughout the year in such magazines as *The World* and *Woman's Journal*. And having thus made the sizeable leap from the *Pall Mall Gazette* to women's weeklies it was not altogether amazing that in April 1887 he should be approached by Thomas Wemyss Reid, the journalist and biographer who was then general manager of the publishing firm of Cassells. In the previous autumn Reid had launched a magazine called *The Lady's World*, a shilling monthly which had not as yet become a marked success, and looking around for ways to improve its circula-tion Reid now hit upon Oscar. Had Wilde not, after all, been a considerable success with the ladies on his many lecture tours? Reid suggested therefore that Oscar should now join him in the editing and reconstructing of the magazine.

It says a good deal for Oscar's catholicity of taste and ambition, as well as for his urgent need of a regular income, that he accepted the job without apparently flinching or hesitating for a moment. *The Lady's World* (one of Oscar's first and foremost achievements there was to have its cover revamped and its title changed to the more popular *The Woman's World*) paid £300 a year and allowed him to continue his freelance activities as well. The lectures were now coming to an end, except for one or two 'special occasions' like the unveiling of a Shakespeare statue at Stratford, but Wilde continued reviewing for the *Pall Mall Gazette* and *The World*, having already published in the latter a scathing attack on Jimmy Whistler when his old friend seemed to be muscling into Oscar's lecture territory. Wilde's jokes about the art world ('On the staircase stood several Royal Academicians disguised as artists') had begun to irritate Whistler, though nothing annoyed him so much as Oscar's piece in the *Pall Mall Gazette* describing the artist as 'a miniature Mephistopheles mocking the majority'. Whistler, ever sensitive about his height, fought back in print: 'What has Oscar in common with art? Except that he dines at our tables and picks from our platter the plums for the pudding he peddles in the provinces.'

It was the end of yet another beautiful friendship, but Oscar was not unduly concerned. *The Woman's World* now promised to take up a considerable amount of his time and energy, and within a few weeks he was its sole editor, Reid having happily reverted to the role of proprietor after Oscar outlined to him plans for the magazine which in essence would not disgrace the editor of a women's monthly in Fleet Street today:

It seems to me that at present [the magazine] is too feminine and not sufficiently womanly. No one appreciates more fully than I do the value and importance of Dress, in its relation to good taste and good health; indeed the subject is one that I have constantly lectured on before Institutes and Societies of various kinds, but it seems to me that the field . . . is to some extent already occupied by such papers as the *Queen* and the *Lady's Pictorial* and that we should take a wider range, as well as a higher standpoint, and deal not merely with what women wear, but with what they think and what they feel. *The Lady's World* should be made the recognized organ for the expression of women's opinions on all subjects of literature, art and modern life, and yet it should be a magazine that men could read with pleasure, and consider it a privilege to contribute to . . . Literary criticism, I think, might be done in the form of paragraphs: that is to say, not from the standpoint of the scholar or the pedant, but from the standpoint of what is pleasant to read; if a book is dull let us say nothing about it, if it is bright let us review it . . . let dress have the end of the magazine; literature, art, travel and social studies at the beginning. Music in a magazine is somewhat dull, no one wants it; a children's column would be much more popular. A popular serial story is absolutely necessary for the start. It need not be by a woman, and should be exciting but not tragic.

The early issues of Oscar's revamped *Woman's World* were a qualified success. He himself contributed the 'literary notes', and he managed to persuade such diverse talents as those of Marie Corelli, Arthur Symons, Helena Sickert, Ouida and

*'If one tells the truth one is sure
sooner or later to be found out': Wilde in 1882.*

Oscar's 'adored and adorable' actresses:
Lily Langtry (left),
Sarah Bernhardt (below left),
and *Ellen Terry* (below).

Wilde in the New World; the fur coat, purchased in Canada, was to last him the rest of his life.

MARRIAGE...

'I am going to be married to a beautiful girl called Constance Lloyd, a grave, slight, violet-eyed little Artemis with great coils of heavy brown hair …and wonderful ivory hands which draw music from the piano so sweet that the birds stop singing to listen to her.' Constance and Oscar were married in 1884. When Oscar went to prison she changed her name to Constance Holland; she died in 1898, a year after his release.

OSCAR WILDE AT WORK
"(IL NE FAVT PAS LE REGARDER)"

FRENCH DICT
AHN'S FIRST COU
DORIAN GRAY
GAUTIER
FAMILY BIBLE
TROIS CONTES
SWINBVRNE
FRENCH VERBS AT A GLANCE

Aubrey Beardsley's classic caricature; 'behind his grotesques',
wrote Wilde, 'there seems to lurk some curious philosophy.'

Above *Oscar seen, fully a year before his
trials, in drag by Alfred Bryan.*

Above right *The first theatrical triumph …
and its star, Marion Terry* (right).

the Queen of Roumania to write as well. He also had no difficulty in soliciting contributions from Constance and the redoubtable Speranza (since his mother was back in action as a poet), though he did get a fair number of refusals, including one from Sarah Bernhardt, who politely declined to have her name at the end of 'A History of My Teagown' even when Oscar promised he would write the piece himself. Undaunted, he then suggested that Sarah should write about her recent American tour, but warned her that his magazine would not care for 'a glorification of the Americans – so they should not be treated as civilized altogether'. Sarah, who planned to tour America again in the near future and saw no good reason to offer gratuitous insults to her prospective audiences there at Oscar's behest, again politely declined.

For the first months of his editorship Oscar was like a child with a new toy. There had always been a great deal of the impresario in him and he worked hard at *The Woman's World*, putting into practice most of the ideas he had outlined to Reid, and dealing tactfully with such contributors as Minnie Simpson, who sent in twenty-thousand-word manuscripts. Travelling every day by train to Fleet Street from Sloane Square, Oscar took to the life of an office commuter with surprising zeal, finding the time at night to continue such private tasks as a collection of fairy stories due to appear in the following year as *The Happy Prince and Other Tales*. Soon however the novelty of editing a magazine began to wear off, as his assistant editor Arthur Fish later recalled:

At first the work was taken quite seriously and 11 o'clock on his appointed morning [Oscar was only committed to three office days a week] saw the poet entering the dingy portals of 'the Yard'; but after a few months his arrival became later and his departure earlier, until at times his visit was little more than a call. After a very short time in my association with him, I could tell by the sound of his approach along the resounding corridor whether the necessary work to be done would be met cheerfully or postponed to a more congenial period. In the latter case he would sink with a sigh into his chair, carelessly glance at his letters, give a perfunctory look at proofs or make-up, ask 'Is it necessary to settle anything today?', put on his hat, and, with a sad 'Good morning', depart again. On his cheerful days, however, everything was different. These were fairly constant in the spring days of the year: there would be a smiling entrance, letters would be answered with epigrammatic brightness, there would be a cheery interval of talk when the work was accomplished, and the dull room would brighten under the influence of his great personality.

The problem for Oscar was that he could scarcely end his days editing women's magazines, and although *The Woman's World* had been a useful stopgap, offering ready money when it was much needed for his young family, it could not be said to be furthering his still resolutely embryonic career in any real way. Nor did he like to think of himself as a journalist, for all that he could be rather good as one; his friends were not to be found among other journalists, nor was he (like his now semi-alcoholic brother Willie) a frequent sight in Fleet Street pubs or clubs. On the other hand, though he was only seven years off the tragedy which was to engulf and effectively end his career, that career had still to find a recognizable form. The 'aesthete' fame had quite gone, and Oscar was now best known as a minor literary and dramatic critic curiously attached to a women's monthly and, as ever, more notable for his personality than for his work.

It was not, Oscar realized, quite enough, nor was it the glittering literary career he had promised himself as far back as Magdalen and Trinity. Yet there was now a clue to where his future reputation would lie, though it was buried deep in 'Lord Arthur Savile's Crime', the short story he had published in *The Court and Society Review* towards the end of 1887. Scattered there, for the first time in any reasonably dramatic shape, could be found a selection of epigrams: 'Not being a genius, he had no enemies.' 'The world is a stage, but the play is badly cast.' 'Surely Providence can resist temptation by this time.' Already, reading these lines, one starts to hear the echoes of those faintly mocking tones that would so soon become the property of Lord Goring, Algernon Moncrieff or John Worthing. The great thing about Wilde was that he stole not only from other writers, but also frequently from himself.

But the first of his four celebrated comedies was still to come, and for the moment Oscar continued to mark time, working on the fairy stories which were to make up his first professionally published book of prose. Arthur Ransome found these 'very married stories – in reading them I cannot help feeling that Wilde wrote one of them as an experiment to show, I suppose, that he could have been Hans Andersen if he'd liked, and his wife then implored him to make a book of things so good, so charming and so true'. More acutely, Hesketh Pearson notes: 'Like all who have expressed themselves in stories or plays for children, from Hans Andersen to James Barrie, he was emotionally undeveloped.' Nevertheless like Peter Pan himself, *The Happy Prince* has worn surprisingly well, and the story – despite a certain flabby vulgarity – was undoubtedly Oscar's first popular success.

Elsewhere at this time Wilde was occupying his mind with such minor diversions as writing to Queen Victoria to ask whether she had any poems suitable for publication in *The Woman's World*. ('Really,' noted Her Majesty, 'what will people not say and invent? Never could the Queen in her whole life write *one line* of *poetry*, serious or comic, or make a *rhyme* ever. This is therefore all *invention* and *myth*.')

But Oscar was bored: bored with the magazine, bored with Constance and the children, and bored with the way in which his own career seemed becalmed in a sea of mediocrity. Occasional domestic dramas such as a brief illness of Cyril's could keep him home in Tite Street, and at such times he was a zealous and exemplary father; more often, however, he would be in search of excuses to leave the house, at one time even convincing Constance that he had to play a game of golf most afternoons. In fact he was in search of something more perilous than a game of golf, and he found it in the eager embrace of a new friend, the seventeen-year-old son of a former Attorney-General of Canada. The young man's name was Robert Baldwin Ross.

7

DORIAN GRAY
AND ALFRED DOUGLAS

—

1888–1891

If Robbie Ross had never existed, Oscar would have had to invent him. The perfect friend, a good conversationalist (many of whose better remarks Oscar sooner or later adopted) and the only man who ever admitted with any real pride to having been Oscar's lover, he became a regular visitor to Tite Street, and even managed for a while to get on reasonably well with Constance, though she later and somewhat acidly noted that he was inclined 'to keep Oscar from his work'.

That cannot have been difficult: Oscar was not, on his own admission, a very devout worker, and it could be argued that his greatest effort at this time was put into his conversations both at home and at the Café Royal. Constance and the boys proving a less than perfect audience, what more natural than that Oscar should have relied on Robbie? When they first met Ross was just seventeen, and Wilde almost twice that age. By all accounts a born personal assistant, Ross was only too happy to disappear into Wilde's ample shadow – emerging when needed to laugh or applaud or argue, but remaining for the rest of the time infinitely self-effacing. In all contemporary accounts of Wilde in later life, Ross is just 'there', loyal and ever-faithful, but only really asserting a character of his own in the immediate aftermath of Oscar's downfall.

Ross had lasted only a year at Cambridge, and when forced by pneumonia to leave he began to make a tentative living as a literary journalist and art historian before ending, some years after Oscar's death, as the Assessor of Picture Valuations to the Board of Trade. Of all Oscar's friends he was undoubtedly the most valuable and at the same time the most inconspicuous – 'a little man', Oscar once called him, probably in tones of patronage rather than criticism, and yet it was almost certainly with Ross (who suitably enough became Oscar's literary executor) that Wilde maintained the steadiest and longest-lasting of all his homosexual affairs.

But Oscar was still the family man: we have Vyvyan's memories, admittedly

hazy, of a conventionally devoted Papa, and although there is one rather un-
nerving account (of Oscar one day asking his sons what they thought happened to
little boys who were naughty and made Mama cry, only to be told by Cyril nothing
so bad as that which happened to 'naughty Papas' who did not come home till
early morning and made Mama cry still more), the atmosphere in the Wilde
family home seems at this time to have been no worse than that in the home of any
other successful Victorian paterfamilias whose work kept him away a good deal
of the time . . . no matter how vaguely 'work' could in Oscar's case be defined.

For a while he persevered with *The Woman's World*, though his appearances in
the office grew fewer and further between. W. E. Henley, the poet and later a
devout Wilde-hater, was also then editing a magazine for the Cassell group, and
once asked Wilde how often he actually went to the office.

'I used to go three times a week for an hour a day, but I have since struck off
one of the days.'

'My God!' exclaimed Henley, 'I went five times a week for five hours a day and
when I wanted to strike off a day they had a special committee meeting.'

'Furthermore,' continued Wilde, 'I never answered their letters. I have known
men come to London full of bright prospects and seen them complete wrecks in a
few months through a habit of answering letters.'

For a while, until Henley began to review Wilde's work unflatteringly, he and
Henley were friends, and it was at Henley's house in London that another Irish
poet had his first meeting with Oscar. W. B. Yeats later recalled:

My first meeting with Oscar Wilde was an astonishment. I had never before heard a
man talking with such perfect sentences, as if he had written them all overnight with
labour and yet all spontaneous. There was present that night at Henley's, by right of
propinquity or of accident, a man full of the secret spite of dullness, who interrupted
from time to time, and always to check or disorder thought; and I noticed with what
mastery he was foiled and thrown. I noticed, too, that the impression of artificiality
that I think all Wilde's listeners have recorded came from the perfect rounding of the
sentences and from the deliberation that made it possible . . . he lived in a little house
in Chelsea . . . perhaps too perfect in its unity, his past of a few years before had gone
too completely, and I remember thinking that the perfect harmony of his life there,
with his beautiful wife and his two young children, suggested some deliberate artistic
composition . . . I remember that he deprecated the very general belief in his success
or his efficiency, and I think with sincerity. One form of success had gone: he was no
more the lion of the season, and he had not discovered his gift for writing comedy, yet
I think I knew him at the happiest moment of his life. No scandal had touched his name,
his fame as a talker was growing among his equals, and he seemed to live in the enjoy-
ment of his own spontaneity.

The years from 1888 to 1892 were very active ones for a man who delighted in
professing his indolence. Continuing his magazine editorship for another year,

until Wemyss Reid grew tired of his non-appearance at the office and replaced him (only to see the entire magazine collapse within another year), Oscar found time to publish half a dozen major essays, another volume of florid children's stories and a collection of short stories, as well as his one and only full-length novel.

The first of the major essays was 'The Decay of Lying' which appeared in the January 1889 number of *The Nineteenth Century*, reappearing alongside most of his other long essays in an anthology called *Intentions* two years later. 'The Decay of Lying' was a dialogue, set in the library of a country house in Nottinghamshire, in which two characters called Cyril and Vivian (but bearing no other discernible similarity to Oscar's own two children) discuss Art, Life and Nature in a rambling conversation which allowed Oscar to lash out at such random and diverse targets as Jimmy Whistler, Rider Haggard and the *Saturday Review* critic who had been less than flattering about *The Happy Prince*. It was followed almost immediately by 'Pen, Pencil and Poison' (first published in the *Fortnightly Review*), an account of Thomas Griffiths Wainewright, the celebrated forger and murderer, for whom Oscar declared a kind of affectionate admiration because 'this young dandy sought to be somebody rather than to do something. He recognized that Life itself is an art, and has its modes of style no less than the arts that seek to express it.'

'Pestilential stuff' St John Ervine thought this, a sure sign that in taking the life and attitudes of a poisoner seriously Oscar himself was already 'dropping down the drain'. At the time however the essay attracted little interest, and in retrospect it can best be seen as a hazy sketch for *Dorian Gray*. 'One can fancy,' wrote Wilde of Wainewright, 'an intense personality being created out of sin.'

Later in the same year came 'The Portrait of Mr W.H.' (published in the July issue of *Blackwood's Edinburgh Magazine*) in which Oscar put forward the theory, lightly disguised in fiction, that the mysterious 'Mr W.H.' to whom Shakespeare's sonnets are dedicated was in fact a young actor called Will Hughes, with whom Shakespeare had in all probability fallen in love. It was not, in 1889, a socially acceptable theory, quite apart from its doubtful authenticity. Frank Harris takes up the story:

'The Portrait of Mr W.H.' did Oscar incalculable injury. It gave his enemies for the first time the very weapon they wanted, and they used it unscrupulously and untiringly with the fierce delight of hatred. Oscar seemed to revel in the storm of conflicting opinions which the paper called forth. He understood better than most men that notoriety is often the forerunner of fame and is always commercially more valuable. He rubbed his hands with delight as the discussion grew bitter, and enjoyed even the sneering of the envious. A wind that blows out a little fire, he knew, plays bellows to a big one. So long as people talked about him, he didn't much care what they said, and they certainly talked interminably about everything he wrote.

But an infinitely greater storm was to break over Oscar's head in the following year, with the publication in *Lippincott's Magazine* of *The Picture of Dorian Gray*.

The magazine had offered Oscar £200 for the serial rights, and the money was more than welcome; having by now lost his regular income from *The Woman's World* his finances were again precarious, as his letter to an income tax inspector that April (1889) indicates: 'I wish your notices were not so agitating and did not hold out such dreadful threats. A penalty of fifty pounds sounds like a relic of mediaeval torture.' A month later he was writing to William Blackwood, agreeing that Blackwood should have the reprint rights to 'The Portrait of Mr W.H.' for £25 but adding hopefully: 'It would be very convenient to me if you would kindly send me a cheque for the story now.'

Now, to the burden of supporting his family and the house in Chelsea, was added that of Speranza, whose legacy from Sir William Wilde was running dangerously low. After some considerable lobbying by Oscar, however (which included writing to the unfortunate Mr Gladstone, who, though now in involuntary possession of all Oscar's published works, still refused to help, which refusal Oscar rewarded by not sending him signed copies of any of his future publications), his mother did get a grant from the Royal Literary Fund of £100, sponsored by Mahaffy, Swinburne and Trevelyan, and a Civil List pension of £70 a year.

But *Dorian Gray* was not written for the money. The idea of a 'major' novel had long appealed to Oscar, whose published work up to this time had been more than a little ephemeral. As early as 1884, he had taken to visiting the studio of a painter friend named Basil Ward, and one day the sitter there was a young man of great beauty who naturally impressed Oscar greatly. 'What a pity,' he said to Ward afterwards, 'that such a glorious creature should ever grow old!' Ward agreed, adding fancifully that it would be wonderful if the boy could always remain young while the portrait aged in his place, and from those slender beginnings, recounted by almost all Wilde's subsequent biographers, was born the outline for *The Picture of Dorian Gray*. Wilde called his artist Basil Hallward as a way of repaying (rather cheaply) the debt to Ward, and Oscar's own philosophy could be heard tumbling from the lips of another character in the book, the exquisite Lord Henry Wotton:

The only way to get rid of temptation is to yield to it; resist it and your soul becomes sick with longing for the things that it has forbidden to itself, with the desire for what its monstrous laws have made monstrous and unlawful ... Be always searching for new sensations. Be afraid of nothing ... Live the wonderful life that is in you ... Conscience and cowardice are really the same things – conscience is the trade name of the firm, that is all.

As if that were not already enough to raise the hackles of Victorian middle-class morality, Oscar added to the hardback version of *Dorian Gray* (ornately illustrated by his friend Charles Ricketts) a preface consisting of twenty-four epigrams ranging from the obvious ('The artist is the creator of beautiful things') to the fatuous ('Thought and language are to the artist instruments of an art') but including the one which, more than anything else Oscar ever said or wrote, was to be held against him in the years ahead: 'There is no such thing as a moral or an immoral book. Books are well written or badly written. That is all.'

Predictably, *Dorian Gray* provoked a gratifying storm of indignation. The book's theatricality and its mass of 'purple patches' (a phrase Oscar claimed as his own) only served to heighten the impression that here was something truly scandalous. Perhaps no other novel of the late nineteenth century, not even *Trilby*, which it preceded by four years, gave rise to such uneasy fascination. 'A tale spawned from the leprous literature of the French decadents,' shrieked the *Daily Chronicle*, while other critics accused Wilde of 'grubbing in muckheaps' and 'tainting young minds'.

'Praise makes me humble,' retorted Oscar, who had a habit of rising to such occasions, 'but when I am abused I know I have touched the stars.' Moreover he had some useful allies: W. B. Yeats found it 'with all its faults a wonderful book', and a number of other critics discovered a strict underlying morality in the story's end. After his years of sinister and voluptuous living, Dorian is after all left on the ground, dead, a figure of senile decay, while the portrait reverts to its original beauty. This moral seems to have been missed, however, by the critic of the *Scots Observer* who complained:

The story – which deals with matters only fitted for the Criminal Investigation Department or a hearing in camera – is discreditable . . . Mr Wilde has brains, and art, and style: but if he can write for none but outlawed noblemen and perverted telegraph boys [a reference to the Lord Arthur Somerset/Cleveland Street homosexual scandal of 1889] the sooner he takes to tailoring or some other decent trade the better for his own reputation and the public morals.

The attacks continued, and Oscar eagerly answered each and every one of them. It was after all good for the sales, and the controversy had raised Oscar overnight from the level of a journalist and fairy-tale composer to that of a vilified author. And had Oscar not already written repeatedly that 'the good fortune of the author is to be misunderstood'? Soon after the story was published in magazine form, Robbie Ross was writing to Wilde: 'Even in the precincts of the Savile nothing but praise of *Dorian Gray* though of course it is said to be very dangerous. I heard a clergyman extolling it; he only regretted some of the sentiments of Lord Henry as apt to lead people astray . . . *Lippincott's* has had a phenomenal sale. Eighty copies were sold in one day at a Strand book-sellers, the usual amount being 3 a week in that part.'

Even Walter Pater, to whose philosophy the book owed so much, was impressed:

We need only emphasize once more the skill, the real subtlety of art, the ease and fluidity withal of one telling a story by word of mouth, with which the consciousness of the supernatural is introduced into, and maintained amid, the elaborately conventional, sophisticated, disabused world Mr Wilde depicts so cleverly, so mercilessly. The special fascination of the piece is of course just there – at that point of contrast. Mr Wilde's work may fairly claim to go with that of Edgar Poe, and with some good French work of the same kind, done, probably, in more or less conscious imitation of it.

Six years later, some of Dorian's lines were to rebound on Oscar with a terrible intensity, but for now the *succès de scandale* restored him to the drawing-rooms of the rich and famous in town and country alike, and to salons the inside of many of which he had not seen since his initial post-Oxford 'aesthete' fame had rubbed off a decade earlier. But the book was to have a more sinister effect on Oscar, as Rupert Croft-Cooke has noted:

From the moment of its publication Oscar seemed to assume the mingled characters of Dorian and Lord Henry. He took to peppering his conversation with wisecracks, to lounging gracefully in long chairs, smoking innumerable cigarettes like Lord Henry and openly indulging his penchant for 'strange sins' like Dorian, or at least posing as one who did, which to Victorian England was nearly as distasteful. The Tite Street householder, the Fleet Street editor, became less and less recognizable in him, and as he advanced towards his fortieth year with growing success, which was to turn to the public triumph of his first modern play, he became over-confident, over-dressed, and overwhelming to all whom he considered his inferiors.

The Picture of Dorian Gray may well be an overblown melodrama, underlaid with more truth than Oscar cared to admit (critics have seen in Hallward traces of Charles Shannon, a real-life artist of the time, and one who had lived with Ricketts; for Wotton the model was thought to be Oscar's old Oxford friend Lord Ronald Gower, though in Dorian himself there were no more than occasional traces of Oscar), but the author was well able to defend both himself and his work. 'Sir,' he wrote to the editor of the *St James's Gazette* on 25 June 1890:

I have read your criticism of my story *The Picture of Dorian Gray* and I need hardly say that I do not propose to discuss its merits or demerits, its personalities or its lack of personality. England is a free country, and ordinary English criticism is perfectly free and easy. Besides, I must admit that, either from temperament or from taste, or from both, I am quite incapable of understanding how any work of art can be criticized from a moral standpoint. The sphere of art and the sphere of ethics are absolutely distinct and separate; and it is to the confusion between the two that we owe the appearance of Mrs Grundy, that amusing old lady who represents the only original form of humour that the middle classes of this country have been able to produce.

The correspondence with the *St James's Gazette* continued for some weeks, since the editor was in the habit of adding abusive replies to the irate letters he printed from Oscar, but all concerned seem to have thoroughly enjoyed the fray, and it was left to historians to note that *Dorian Gray* was the first overtly pederastic novel (Basil admits his love for Dorian, who is then lured away by the wicked

Lord Henry) since the *Satyricon*. But its survival into the twentieth century (like
that of *Trilby*) depends on nothing more furtive than an essentially workable plot:
MGM filmed it in 1945 (with George Sanders as Wotton) and thirty years later
John Osborne, having turned it into a stage play, explained his own lifelong
fascination with the novel:

> I remember reading it as a boy of about eleven and it went a long way towards
> dispelling the fatty image of those fairy stories which I had read earlier and which
> offended a small ulcerous reticence within me even then . . . the fact remains that *The*
> *Picture of Dorian Gray* is not only a remarkable achievement of its time, given all its
> faults, but the germinal story is an inspired one like, say, that of Jekyll and Hyde. The
> story itself is what sold out the issues of *Lippincott's* and intrigued its Victorian
> readers. It is a variation on the Mephistophelian bargain with the devil . . . one of the
> things that has struck me about the original book is its feeling of wilful courage and
> despair, the two qualities only too clearly embodied in the spirit of Wilde himself. It is
> an infuriating work, often misleading, sometimes deadly serious when it should be self-
> mocking, and so on. For example, there was a time some years ago when the ethic of
> effortless physical beauty might have seemed no more than a camp, tiresomely self-
> abusing piece of attitudinizing. But today? What are the things most valued, sought
> after? Beauty, yes; youth, most certainly . . . it is obligatory to be trim, slim, careless.
> The lines of age on Dorian Gray's portrait are a very modern likeness in all this . . .
> what prolongs active life? Why, a shot of Dorian Grays! Dorian Grays to you, man.

In the nine months which separated the magazine from the hardback publication
of *Dorian Gray*, Oscar published the two parts of the dialogue essay entitled 'The
Critic as Artist', as well as 'The Soul of Man under Socialism' and two collections
of his earlier essays and stories. In the nine months following the hardback
publication he also published another collection of children's stories (*The House of*
Pomegranates), making this 1888-91 period the most prolific of his entire career.
'The Critic as Artist' (published with 'some remarks upon the importance of
doing nothing') consisted of a duologue between two characters now called Gilbert
and Ernest and located in the library of a house overlooking Green Park. In their
lighter moments of conversation there are faint, shadowy outlines of Oscar's
beginnings as a comic dramatist, but the fundamental thesis here was that criticism
is a kind of spiritual autobiography, having much more to do with the critic than
with the thing criticized. But, as in 'The Decay of Lying', the conversation of the
two characters – neither was given any kind of descriptive background beyond a
name – was allowed and indeed encouraged to ramble over such widely varied
topics as Wordsworth ('He went to the lakes but he was never a Lake Poet – he
found in stones the sermons he had already hidden there.'), Meredith ('Meredith
is a prose Browning. So is Browning.') and war ('As long as war is regarded as
wicked it will always have its fascination. When it is looked upon as vulgar, it
will cease to be popular').

'The Soul of Man under Socialism' was an altogether more serious affair. Wilde's only social tract, it appeared in a February 1891 issue of the *Fortnightly Review*, and was supposed to have been sparked off by an address on Socialism given by Bernard Shaw at Westminster, for which Wilde was in the audience. GBS himself seemed somewhat uncertain ('Robert Ross surprised me greatly by telling me long after Oscar's death that it was this address of mine that moved Oscar to try his hand at a similar feat') and, if Ross is right, the essay is one of surprisingly few links between the two men. Though born within two years of each other in Dublin, and though both were destined to become unarguably the best-known playwrights in the English language after Shakespeare, the two men seem to have had curiously little in common, and indeed to have had curiously little interest in each other. True, Wilde was kind about *Widowers' Houses* at a time when nobody else was, and Shaw repaid the compliment by writing thoughtfully and generously about Wilde's plays in the aftermath of the scandal, at a time when precious few others would even mention Wilde's name. But asked years later by Frank Harris to list his meetings with Wilde, Shaw could only come up with five, apart from the possibility of his Westminster speech. There had been two early meetings in Dublin, and there were to be three more at the height of Oscar's play-writing fame, though, Shaw recalled: 'Our queer shyness of one another made our resolutely cordial and appreciative conversation so difficult that our final laugh and shake-hands was almost a reciprocal confession.'

Bernard Partridge, however, recollects another occasion:

I was present at their meeting in the rooms of the late Fitzgerald Molloy in Red Lion Square. There were only the four of us. Shaw was on the threshold of his career; Oscar had already 'arrived'. But for once he was content to listen, and Shaw, delighted to meet such a listener, let himself go. His subject was a magazine, the founding of which he had in mind, and he held forth at great length on its scope and outlook. When he came to a halt, Oscar said 'That has all been most interesting, Mr Shaw; but there's one point you haven't mentioned, and an all-important one – you haven't told us the title of your magazine.' 'Oh, as for that' said Shaw, 'what I'd want to do would be to impress my own personality on the public – I'd call it "Shaw's Magazine": Shaw-Shaw-Shaw!' and he banged his fist on the table. 'Yes' said Oscar, 'and how would you spell it?'

Wilde's brand of socialism, as expressed in his essay, is unsurprisingly rather different from that of George Bernard Shaw. So far from being either Fabian or State-enthused, Oscar's pamphlet advocates a kind of romantic individualism and an improvement in the lot of the workers, the latter to be achieved not through money but through the arts – educate the barbarians, he wrote, and they will cease to be barbarians. He also concluded: 'Man has sought to live intensely, fully, perfectly. When he can do so without exercising restraint over others, or suffering it ever, and his activities are all pleasurable to him, he will be saner, healthier, more civilized, more himself. Pleasure is Nature's test, her sign of approval. When man is happy, he is in harmony with himself and his environment.'

Oscar also admitted the wild impracticalities of most of the theories expressed in his essay, though that did not save him from the wrath of the establishment, which viewed any attempt at an improvement of the workers' lot, no matter how romantic, as sheer heresy. 'All these literary bullets,' commented *The Spectator*, 'are shot out in defence of the thesis that men should be themselves, in contempt, it would seem, not merely of the public, but of all law which restricts their individualism. The article, if serious, would be thoroughly unhealthy, but it leaves on us the impression of being written merely to startle and excite talk.'

By those who had not troubled to read him with much care – and they were in a sizeable majority – Oscar was thus regarded now as a libertine and a socialist, two of the most awful epithets in the upper-middle-class Victorian dictionary. Still more irritatingly, he was clearly a success, and, with that success, showed no signs of mellowing or quieting down but instead became noisier and more flamboyant by the month. He was, to put it mildly, riding for a fall, and it was in mid-gallop towards it that he met the young Lord Alfred Douglas.

Precisely how they met is now chronicled in some detail: early in 1890, on one of his periodic visits to Oxford where he used to find the atmosphere and the young men equally seductive, Oscar had met up with a Wykehamist called Lionel Johnson, then up at New College. 'He discourses with infinite flippancy of everyone,' wrote Johnson later, 'laughs at Pater and consumes all my cigarettes. I am in love with him.' Within a few months, however, Johnson seems to have been cheerfully introducing Oscar to other young men, and in January 1891 he took with him to see Wilde, at Tite Street, Lord Alfred Bruce Douglas, then in his second year at Magdalen.

Douglas was just twenty-one. The third son of the eighth Marquis of Queensberry, he had been educated at Winchester too, but had led a somewhat disturbed early childhood. The eighth Marquis, being seldom in total control of his senses, had managed to lose more than half the £700,000 estate which he had inherited from the seventh Marquis, and although he was assured of a place in history for having compiled the rules of boxing which were forever to bear his name (he himself had been a former amateur lightweight champion), his own family held him in rather more dubious regard. He was, according to Hesketh Pearson:

... extremely combative, self-assertive, prejudiced, and conceited, and would go to any lengths to revenge what he construed as an insult. Indifference to his views drove him frantic; and as he bored people with his atheistical opinions on every possible occasion, he was frequently driven frantic. He may have been liked by his horses and dogs, with whom he spent far more time than with his wife and children, but no one else cared for him and most of his acquaintances were frightened of him. On the rare occasions when he was at home he bullied his wife and neglected his children, but nearly all his time was spent elsewhere and Douglas says that as a boy he scarcely ever saw his father. Once the entire family were turned out of their home near Ascot at twenty-four hours' notice because Queensberry wished to bring a party of friends which included his mistress.

Lady Queensberry had eventually had enough of the 'mad Marquis'. In 1887, four years before Oscar first met her son, she had divorced him, and in so doing started a battle for alimony which was to last almost to the end of her days. Nor were Queensberry's quarrels reserved exclusively for his ex-wife: his second marriage was annulled after only six months, and before his third son's liaison with Oscar offered such an inviting target he spent much of his time attacking the two older sons, one for accepting an English peerage and the other for marrying a clergyman's daughter.

Douglas's family background thus had all the makings of a good Whitehall farce. That he himself had become involved in a bad gothic tragedy was only to become apparent some time later.

8
LADY WINDERMERE...
AND SALOMÉ

—

1891–1892

Oscar's new-found friendship with 'Bosie' Douglas (a corruption of his childhood nickname Boysie) began slowly. The young man was a poet, a Lord and an athlete, all except the last of which appealed to Oscar, and he was also immensely good-looking. But there were other such good-looking young men in Oscar's life at the time, albeit none of comparable nobility, and Douglas does not appear in any of Oscar's letters until May or June of 1892, by which time, admittedly, Wilde was informing Robbie Ross (who cannot have been best pleased) that Bosie was 'like a narcissus – so white and gold'.

But for the rest of 1891 Oscar was content to leave Bosie at Magdalen. His own career was again at something of an impasse, since he had by now published almost all the essays, poems and children's stories he was ever going to write, and had no apparent desire to start on a novel to follow *Dorian Gray*. Yet there was something else at the back of his mind: it had been seven years now since the failure of *Vera* on Broadway had turned his attention indignantly away from the theatre, and although *The Duchess of Padua* had been briefly and anonymously produced in New York at the height of his *Dorian Gray* publicity in England, Oscar had written nothing for the theatre since 1883.

In 1890 he had, however, begun to think seriously about playwriting once again, largely at the insistence of his old friend Norman Forbes-Robertson, who was about to take over the management of the Globe Theatre and was therefore in urgent need of plays. Forbes-Robertson even agreed to pay Oscar an advance of £100, but his play never materialized; nor did a still less likely Bernard Partridge project whereby Oscar was to put together a pantomime for the Lyceum ('only if they'd let me dramatize the Book of Revelations'). However, by the beginning of February 1891 Oscar was writing to George Alexander, then already managing the St James's, about an idea which was to become the first of his four great stage comedies, *Lady Windermere's Fan*:

I am not satisfied with myself or my work. I can't get a grip of the play yet; I can't get my people real. The fact is I worked at it when I was not in the mood for work, and must first forget it, and then go back quite fresh to it. I am very sorry, but artistic work can't be done unless one is in the mood; certainly my work can't. Sometimes I spend months over a thing, and don't do any good; at other times I write a thing in a fortnight.

In fact it was to be another full year before *Lady Windermere's Fan* reached the stage: a year which Oscar spent in London and Paris working on the script and writing amorous letters to such now-established friends as Richard le Gallienne: 'I want so much to see you: when can that be? Friendship and love like ours need not meetings, but they are delightful. I hope the laurels are not too thick across your brow [le Gallienne had just published a book about Meredith] for me to kiss your eyelids.'

Oscar had evidently decided by now that he was to become once again a man of the theatre. He even tried to unload *The Duchess of Padua* on to Henry Irving, who politely declined it despite being assured by Oscar of its 'immense success' (as *Guido Ferranti*) in New York, where it in fact had lasted less than three weeks. But Oscar had by now another advance – this one from Alexander – under his belt, and with the money he went to Paris for a spring 'recuperation'.

Back in England he retreated to a cottage near Lake Windermere and there, within about a month, completed the story of Lady Windermere, whose suspicions are aroused when her husband asks her to invite a certain Mrs Erlynne to her twenty-first birthday ball. In fact Mrs Erlynne turns out to be Lady Windermere's divorced mother, and is secretly blackmailing Lord Windermere into facilitating her return to polite society after a continental affair. When she arrives at the ball, Lady Windermere (still not recognizing her mother) is all set to go off with her admirer Lord Darlington in a fit of jealousy. Mrs Erlynne follows her and persuades Lady Windermere to return to her husband and family, but she has left her fan behind and Mrs Erlynne has to persuade the now suspicious Lord Windermere that the fan was borrowed by her and that there is therefore no reason why it should not have been found at Lord Darlington's. This she does, before Act Four reveals all and mother, daughter and husband are tearfully reunited in time for the final curtain.

Triumphantly, Oscar returned to London with his play and sent it to George Alexander under its then title *A Good Woman*. He also took the precaution of sending another copy to Augustin Daly, the Broadway manager, but Alexander's enthusiasm was immediate and warm. Oscar had described his script as 'one of those modern drawing-room plays with pink lampshades' and Alexander saw that it combined Wilde's by now celebrated and familiar gift for the epigram with enough of a dramatic situation to satisfy those already accustomed to the 'problem plays' of the time. Indeed, so confident was Alexander of its success that he offered to buy the play for £1000 outright, but his enthusiasm warned Oscar that there might be even more money to be made out of *Lady Windermere's Fan*, so he held out for a profit-sharing deal, one which eventually made him seven times as much as Alexander's original offer.

But *Lady Windermere's Fan* was not due to go into rehearsal at the St James's for another six months, and in the meantime Oscar took himself back to his beloved Paris, pausing only to fight off some more Press attacks, this time in connection with his second collection of fairy stories, which were widely regarded as more than a little unsuitable, not to say top-heavy, for their apparent audience. 'In building this *House of Pomegranates*,' retorted Oscar, 'I had about as much intention of pleasing the British child as I had of pleasing the British public.'

In Paris he met Stéphane Mallarmé (to whom he gave a copy of *Dorian Gray*), the actor Coquelin and the playwright Pierre Louÿs, to say nothing of the Ranee of Sarawak, the Princess of Monaco and (again) Edmond de Goncourt. In their heady company he continued to work on *Salomé*, a one-act tragedy begun a few months earlier in the rather less exalted surroundings of Torquay, where he was briefly holidaying with Constance and the children. The play (written originally in French and only translated into English some years later by Alfred Douglas) would, Oscar hoped, secure his election to the Académie Française; in fact it did nothing of the kind, nor was it (as later rumour had it) conceived as a vehicle for Sarah Bernhardt.

In fact the legends that have grown up around *Salomé* are nearly as exotic as the piece itself. By far the most colourful is Vincent O'Sullivan's description of Oscar sitting down to write it in a blank exercise book that he had happened upon after a particularly good Parisian lunch. Finding himself still writing at eleven that night, Oscar goes into a nearby café, orders a meal and sends for the orchestra leader. 'I am,' says Oscar, 'writing a play about a woman dancing in her bare feet in the blood of a man she has craved for and slain. I want you to play something in harmony with my thoughts.' In any event *Salomé* (complete with Herod and Herodias and Jokanaan and the Dance of the Seven Veils) was finished by the time Oscar got back to London in the late autumn of 1891. He now had two complete but unproduced plays under his belt, and was eagerly awaiting the start of Alexander's rehearsals at the St James's.

These did not go as smoothly as might have been expected. Alexander felt that the playwright was too much in evidence, not only in rehearsal but also in the play itself. The actor-manager was playing the comparatively minor role of Windermere, which gave him more than enough time to notice certain faults of overwriting and over-elaborate plotting. Lily Hanbury was cast as Lady Windermere, with Marion Terry as the scandalous Mrs Erlynne and Ben Webster as Cecil Graham. Alexander himself was directing, and in rehearsal there were jovial references to 'the Oscar Wilde Epigram and Paradox Company, Limited', but the company was determined that this was going to be something more than an evening with Mr Wilde's witticisms. At the end of Act Two, Alexander felt, Mrs Erlynne should reveal her secret, thereby converting 'a riddle' into 'a play of real emotion and suspense'. Wilde at first refused the alteration, ending his letter somewhat ominously:

I have built my house on a certain foundation, and this foundation cannot be altered. I can say no more. With regard to matters personal between us, I trust that tonight [the opening performance] will be quite harmonious and peaceful. After the play is produced and before I leave for the South of France where I am obliged to go for my health, it might be wise for us to have at any rate one meeting for the purpose of explanation.

The Wilde-Alexander relationship was smoothed over, however, and Oscar did agree to make the change after the first night, allowing Mrs Erlynne's secret to be revealed in Act Two as Alexander had asked. But by then, Oscar was acting from strength: the first night at the St James's, 20 February 1892, had been an un-qualified public success for the author. As the final curtain fell, to thunderous cries of 'Oscar!' he had strolled onto the stage with a lighted cigarette in his hand and in his buttonhole a green carnation – the flower which was, from that night onward until the trials, to be the badge for Oscar and his followers just as it was the badge for homosexuals in Paris at the time. 'Ladies and Gentlemen,' said Oscar, 'I have enjoyed this evening immensely. The actors have given us a charming rendering of a delightful play, and your appreciation has been most intelligent. I congratulate you on the great success of your performance, which persuades me that you think almost as highly of the play as I do.'

The audience was delighted; the critics, those who had not already left to start writing their reviews, horrified. 'People of birth and breeding don't do such things,' said Clement Scott in the words of Ibsen's Judge Brack, and other critics were divided in their reviews. William Archer and Walkley both thoroughly approved of the play, Joseph Knight did not. *Black and White* magazine thought it:

. . . obvious that Mr Wilde regards a play merely as a vehicle for the expression of epigram and the promulgation of paradox. *Lady Windermere's Fan* is not really a play; it is a pepper-box of paradoxes. The piece is improbable without being interesting . . . Mr Wilde's figures talk a Back Slang of their own; once accept the conditions of the game, and the fantastic becomes the familiar. Black is white, day is night; well and good by all means. But what next? While it is fresh, however, this kind of fantasy is exceedingly diverting; and its humours are interpreted at the St James's after a fashion which must surely temper Mr Wilde's disdain for actors.

Punch, predictably, leapt on Oscar's curtain speech with a cartoon labelled 'Quite Too-Too Puffickly Precious!!' and subtitled 'Lady Windy-mère's Fan-cy Portrait of the new dramatic author, Shakespeare Sheridan Oscar Puff, Esq'. Surrounding the drawing was a page-long parody of the play itself, complete with characters called 'Earl Pennyplaine' and 'Lord Tuppence Cullard', to say nothing of the 'Duchess of Battersea'. They even parodied Oscar's curtain speech, ending it hopefully:

AUTHOR: . . . I repeat, as I have to catch a train – I repeat, as I have to catch a train . . .
ENTIRE AUDIENCE: And so have we! (Exeunt. Thus the play ends in smoke.)

In fact the play ran on at the St James's until the end of 1892, with the interval of a short provincial tour, and it established Oscar swiftly and comparatively painlessly as the leading comic dramatist of his time. Some critics liked to suggest that anyone could have come up with the best lines in the play ('So far as I can discover,' wrote Bernard Shaw, 'I am the only person in London who cannot sit down and write an Oscar Wilde comedy at will'), but the fact remains that only Oscar had done so, and the play became the hit of the season. 'Royalty,' Oscar told a friend proudly, 'are turned away nightly,' and a musical parody called *The Poet and The Puppets* was performed later in the year with Charles Hawtrey in the lead. The 'poet' of the title was of course Oscar, who had caused considerable indignation with a speech to the Playgoer's Club unfavourably comparing his cast to 'puppets'.

Oscar's brother Willie had written one of the play's less favourable reviews, but by now Oscar was past caring ('After a good dinner,' he once said, 'one can forgive anybody anything, even one's own relations'), and Bernard Shaw added his praise when he became a drama critic a year or two later. *Lady Windermere's Fan* was Alexander's first big success at the St James's, although Wilde was anxious to prevent too much credit going his way and fervently denied in print that the alterations to the play had been made at his exclusive suggestion. But taken all in all Wilde's was the first major English stage comedy since *The School For Scandal* more than a hundred years earlier, and as he himself noted rather smugly in *De Profundis*: 'I took the drama, the most objective form known to art, and made of it as personal a mode of expression as the lyric or the sonnet; at the same time I widened its range and enriched its characterization.'

Wilde ought by rights to have had two plays running in London during the summer of 1892. By this time he had again met his French idol Sarah Bernhardt, who had asked (in the light of Oscar's new-found success as a playwright) whether he had anything suitable for her. Inevitably he gave her *Salomé* and by mid-June she had it already in London rehearsal, with scenery being designed by W. Graham Robertson ('Tell me,' demanded Oscar, 'are we to call you W or Graham?'). But hearing of it, and backed by a medieval law designed to suppress Catholic Mystery plays, the Lord Chamberlain stepped in and had the production halted. La Bernhardt was understandably furious over the waste of her time and money;

Oscar, espying yet another potential *cause célèbre*, leapt into the fray and announced that in his outrage at such censorship he would be giving up his British citizenship and going to live in France. He protested to *The World*:

The censorship apparently regards the stage as the lowest of all the arts, and looks on acting as a vulgar thing. The painter is allowed to take his subjects where he chooses ... the sculptor is equally free ... And the writer, the poet, he is also quite free ... But there is a Censorship over the stage and acting; and the basis of that Censorship is that, while vulgar subjects may be put on the stage and acted, while everything that is mean and low and shameful in life can be portrayed by actors, no actor is to be permitted to present under artistic conditions the great and ennobling subjects taken from the Bible. The insult in the suppression of Salomé is an insult to the stage as a form of art, and not to me.

Soon afterwards he explained to the London correspondent of the Parisian daily *Le Gaulois* the reasons for his decision to emigrate:

My resolution is deliberately taken. Since it is impossible to have a work of art performed in England, I shall transfer myself to another fatherland of which I have long been enamoured ... Moreover I am not at present an Englishman. I am an Irishman, which is by no means the same thing. No doubt I have English friends to whom I am deeply attached; but as to the English, I do not love them. There is a great deal of hypocrisy in England which you in France very rightly find fault with. The typical Briton is Tartuffe seated in his shop behind the counter. There are numerous exceptions, but they only prove the rule.

Had he carried out his threat, it has been argued, Oscar would never have had to face the terrible indignities of 1895, and his career might have worked out altogether differently. In that case we might have gained from him more *Salomés* but we would also have in all probability lost *The Importance of Being Earnest*; in any event, there is good reason to believe that what he was involved in here was a grand gesture rather than a real decision. *Punch* took him up on it as usual, and cartooned him in the uniform of a French soldier, but the banning of *Salomé* also brought forth a splendid letter in his defence written to the *Pall Mall Gazette* by William Archer:

Ever since Mr Oscar Wilde told me, a fortnight ago, that his *Salomé* had been accepted by Madame Sarah Bernhardt I have been looking forward with a certain malign glee, to the inevitable suppression of the play ... but it is surely unworthy of Mr Wilde's lineage to turn tail and run away from a petty tyranny which lives upon the disunion and apathy of English dramatic authors. Paris does not particularly want Mr Wilde. There he would be one talent among many, handicapped moreover, in however slight a degree, by having to use an acquired idiom ... Here on the other hand Mr Wilde's talent is unique. We require it and we appreciate it – those of us, at any rate, who are capable of any sort of artistic appreciation.

In the end Oscar showed no sign of being about to leave for France, though he did set off for a brief holiday in Bad Homburg in the company of Alfred Douglas, there to take the waters. By this time they were a near-inseparable couple, their friendship having been confirmed one night after a performance of *Lady Windermere's Fan* when they returned to Tite Street where, with Constance and the children away, Oscar seduced the young Lord. In later life, however, Douglas was keen to establish the boundaries of their relations. In one of his most hilarious circumlocutions he noted in 1929 that in his affair with Oscar: 'Of the sin which takes its name from one of the Cities of the Plain there was never the slightest question. I give this as my solemn word before God, as I hope to be saved. What there was, was quite bad enough. But, as I have already remarked, when all this happened I had been six years at school and at Oxford, and I had lost my moral sense and had no religion.'

Since their first encounter a year earlier the two men had not often met, and Oscar had indeed been living intermittently with Edward Shelley, an office boy at the publishing house of John Lane and Elkin Mathews 'at the Bodley Head', where they had just reprinted his collected *Poems*. It was Shelley to whom Wilde sent the best first-night tickets for *Lady Windermere's Fan*, but in the hour of his greatest triumph with that play he had renewed the acquaintance with Bosie, who had by now got himself into trouble with an Oxford 'renter', a semi-professional homosexual who first allowed Bosie to seduce him and then began to demand money for his silence.

Money, for the first time in his life, was what Oscar now had, and he cheerfully bought Bosie out of his dilemma with the help of a lawyer called George Lewis. This was by no means the first or last of Bosie's homosexual difficulties at Oxford (one of which caused him to leave the university somewhat abruptly at the end of his final year, without taking a degree), but it was the first real bond between the two men. Their friendship then moved swiftly towards an intensity which was to dominate the next three years of Oscar's life.

But immediately after the *Salomé* furore he had begun to think about another play: not, this time, for George Alexander (the quarrel about Act Two of *Lady Windermere's Fan* having severely dented their alliance), but for another of London's actor-managers, Herbert Beerbohm Tree, then in control of the Haymarket Theatre. Wilde and Tree got along considerably better than Wilde and Alexander. Tree was altogether more flamboyant, and moreover he regarded Oscar as 'a great gentleman', while for his part Oscar noted proudly that: 'Every day dear Herbert becomes "de plus en plus Oscarisé" – it is a wonderful case of Nature imitating Art.' Their mutual admiration even survived an uneasy moment when Tree announced that he would be playing the lead in Oscar's new piece, only to be told by the author: 'As Herod in my *Salomé* you would be admirable: as a Peer of the Realm in my latest device, pray forgive me if I do not see you.'

Nevertheless it was for Tree and the Haymarket that Oscar began to write *A Woman of No Importance* in the late summer of 1892. To do so, he took himself and Constance and the boys to Babbacombe in Dorset, having finalized arrangements with Mathews and Lane at the Bodley Head for the reprint of his *Poems*. A letter written by Oscar at this time to John Lane, referring to a contract they had just signed for Oscar's new poem 'The Sphinx' (to be published two years later), gives some idea of Oscar's own appreciation of his professional standing, and of his still acute sense of public relations:

I return to you the agreement signed and witnessed. I have made some alterations in it. The maker of a poem is a 'poet', not an 'author': author is misleading.

Also the selection of reviews to which the book is sent must be a matter of arrangement between you and your partner and me. A book of this kind – very rare and curious – must not be thrown into the gutter of English journalism. No book of mine, for instance, ever goes to the *National Observer*. I wrote to Henley to tell him so, two years ago. He is too coarse, too offensive, too personal, to be sent any work of mine. I hope that the book will be subscribed for before publication, and that as few as possible will be sent for review . . . no such thing as a popular or a cheap edition is to be brought out; nor are you to be able to assign the right of publishing the poem to any other firm.

The house at Babbacombe, which Oscar took from Lady Mount-Temple on a three-month lease for £100, was a great success despite some early misgivings ('Are there beautiful people in London?' he wrote in anguish to Robbie Ross. 'Here there are none – everyone is so unfinished'), and Wilde grew so attached to it that when Constance went off to Italy for a visit he stayed there with his two sons and invited Bosie to join them. This somewhat bizarre *ménage à quatre* remained there throughout the winter, Oscar growing daily more devoted to Bosie ('He is very gilt-haired and I have bound *Salomé* in purple to suit him'). They even devised a joky timetable for what had now, presumably on account of Cyril and Vyvyan, become known as 'Babbacombe School': the 'Headmaster' was to be Oscar himself, the 'Second Master' an Oxford undergraduate called Campbell Dodgson, who had also been staying with them, and the 'Boys' were to be Lord Alfred Douglas:

Rules.

Tea for masters and boys at 9.30 a.m.
Breakfast at 10.30.
Work. 11.30–12.30.
At 12.30 Sherry and biscuits for headmaster and boys (the second master objects to this).
12.40–1.30. Work.
1.30. Lunch.
2.30–4.30. Compulsory hide-and-seek for headmaster.

5. Tea for headmaster and second master, brandy and sodas (not to exceed seven) for boys.

6–7. Work.

7.30. Dinner, with compulsory champagne.

8.30–12. Écarté, limited to five-guinea points.

12.–1.30. Compulsory reading in bed. Any boy found disobeying this rule will be immediately woken up.

Though immersed in *A Woman of No Importance* for much of his time at Babba-combe, Oscar took the trouble to write to Bernard Shaw applauding him for his book on Ibsen, a courageously unfashionable thing to do; and though Bosie had by now become the centre of his attention he still maintained his ties with such other 'close friends' as the actor Sydney Barraclough and the poet John Gray, whose work Oscar paid the Bodley Head to publish in a volume called *Silverpoints*. Nonetheless it was Bosie with whom Oscar was now infatuated and to whom (after he had returned to London and posted Wilde one of his poems) Oscar wrote the letter which was to be stolen later, then used in attempted blackmail of Wilde, and finally read out at his trials:

My Own Boy, Your sonnet is quite lovely, and it is a marvel that those red rose-leaf lips of yours should have been made no less for music of song than for madness of kisses. Your slim gilt soul walks between passion and poetry. I know Hyacinthus, whom Apollo loved so madly, was you in Greek days.

That letter, written almost certainly in the January of 1893 from Babbacombe Cliff, was in its way the beginning of the end.

9
A WOMAN OF NO IMPORTANCE...
AND SOME PANTHERS
OF CONSIDERABLE SIGNIFICANCE

—

1893–1894

Returning to London from Babbacombe, Oscar gave *A Woman of No Importance* to Beerbohm Tree, who put it into almost immediate rehearsal at the Haymarket. The second of Wilde's four great social comedies, it has worn least well, perhaps because of a plot which fairly creaks along, seeming to owe rather more to Pinero than to the great comic talent which was to sustain Wilde from *Lady Windermere's Fan* through to *The Importance of Being Earnest* three years later.

The 'woman of no importance' is a Mrs Arbuthnot, once mistress to Lord Illingworth, but now forgotten until a handsome young man applies for the job of his social secretary. The man is in fact their son, Gerald Arbuthnot, but the truth is only revealed to his father by Mrs Arbuthnot after Lord Illingworth has attempted to steal Gerald's fiancée. The play ends with Illingworth's insufferably patronizing farewell to Mrs Arbuthnot, and her subsequent dismissal of him as 'a man of no importance'.

Max Beerbohm thought this 'the most truly dramatic' of all Wilde's plays, and believed that had he continued in its vein he could well have been a playwright of more substantial importance to the development of drama in the 1890s. But the play's chief interest now (apart from some stirringly anti-British speeches delivered by Gerald's American fiancée) lies in Wilde's handling of class warfare, an issue he treats seriously but somehow unconvincingly, like the perpetually detached observer he and his leading male characters in each play were always to be. He also seemed unable to put any real conviction into the problem of Gerald's illegitimacy, though at one unforgettable moment he does have Mrs Arbuthnot cry: 'Child of my shame, be still the child of my shame!'

Tree, no stranger to theatricality himself (and the actor who was later to take on both Svengali and Professor Higgins), accepted the plot with evident delight, however, and directed it himself, as was then the custom of the actor-managers.

With hindsight it could be supposed that what really interested Wilde about his own play was the developing relationship between Gerald and Lord Illingworth before they discover they are father and son, but this was not an issue on which the bluff, hearty Tree could bring himself to dwell.

He himself was playing Illingworth, with Fred Terry as Gerald (a part Oscar had tried, and failed, to get for his friend Barraclough) and Mrs Bernard Beere as Mrs Arbuthnot. Others in the cast included Holman Clark and (as the fiancée) a young Julia Neilson, later of course to marry her stage fiancé Fred Terry. The script featured rather fewer of the epigrams which had been the hallmark and the making of *Lady Windermere's Fan*, but Oscar still noted proudly that the first act contained 'absolutely no action at all – it is a perfect act'.

As rehearsals progressed, Wilde and Tree had the inevitable falling-out (not, this time, over script changes but over who was ultimately to be in charge of the production, a battle Tree won by the simple expedient of being in charge of the theatre where it was being staged), and Oscar was for a while banned from the building. Later however these differences were patched up, and Tree's young half-brother Max Beerbohm subsequently recalled:

During rehearsals we used to go to a little bar around the corner where they served sandwiches. Oscar asked for a watercress sandwich. When the waiter brought it, it seemed to Oscar excessive. 'I asked for a watercress sandwich,' he said to the waiter – in the friendliest manner possible, smiling at him as if asking for, and being sure of, the waiter's sympathy – 'not for a loaf of bread with a field in the middle of it.'

All was not as well as it might have been between Oscar and Bosie at this time: the first flush of their friendship had paled, and from the Savoy Hotel, where he was staying during rehearsals, Oscar wrote:

Bosie, you must not make scenes with me. They kill me, they wreck the loveliness of life. I cannot see you, so Greek and gracious, distorted with passion, I cannot listen to your curved lips saying hideous things to me. I would sooner be blackmailed by every renter in London than have you bitter, unjust, hating. I must see you soon. You are the divine thing I want, the thing of grace and beauty . . .

The tiff soon forgotten, Oscar returned to *A Woman of No Importance*, but there was now a more serious problem on the horizon, also relating to Bosie. During this last year of his at Oxford, he had taken a youth called Alfred Wood to live with him there. Wood was already known to be more than a little light-fingered but Bosie made him a number of presents, including a suit of his clothes, in the pocket of which he had carelessly left the 'slim gilt soul' letter that Oscar had written him from Babbacombe. Back in London, Wood took the letter along to Oscar, who was not at all worried but much struck by Wood himself, whom he took back to Tite Street for the night before giving him enough money to sail for America. But Wood had also shown the letter to two professional blackmailers called Cliburn and Allen, who made copies of it and sent one to Beerbohm Tree at the Haymarket.

Tree, more than a little horrified but not knowing quite what the form was in such cases as this, passed the copy back to Oscar with a warning that he should be more careful. Allen then appeared in person, demanding £10 for the original and assuring Oscar that he had been offered £60 for it elsewhere. Oscar told Allen that he should have taken the money, as it was 'an extremely beautiful letter and I am glad to find there is someone in England willing to pay so large a sum for a work of mine'. Allen, thoroughly confused by now and realizing that Wilde was not after all going to be an easy touch, sent Cliburn back to Tite Street with the original letter, and Oscar took it, giving him ten shillings for all his trouble and adding: 'I am afraid you are leading a desperately wicked life.'

Clearly at this time Oscar thought of himself not as an unhappy deviant whose sexual tastes and habits put him at the mercy of every alert renter in London, but instead as an all-powerful artist able to go his own way in his sex life as elsewhere, and to rise above such vulgarities as blackmail. And, for the time being, that was true.

The first night of *A Woman of No Importance*, 19 April 1893, was an unqualified success. Max described it in a letter to his friend Reggie Turner:

I could not see a single nonentity in the whole house ... Balfour and Chamberlain and all the politicians were there. When little Oscar came to make his bow there was a slight mingling of hoots and hisses, though he looked very sweet in a new white waistcoat and a large bunch of little lilies in his coat. The notices are better than I had expected: the piece is sure of a long, of a very long run, despite all that the critics may say in its favour. Last night I went again ... after the play I supped with Oscar and Alfred Douglas (who is staying with him) and my brother at the Albemarle ... he told us one lovely thing. A little journalist who had several times attacked him vulgarly came up to him in the street the other day and cordially accosted him. Oscar stared at him and said after a moment or two: 'You will pardon me: I remember your name perfectly, but I can't recall your face.'

Mindful of the controversy over his curtain speech from the stage on the first night of *Lady Windermere's Fan*, Oscar limited himself on this occasion to a bow from the box, after which he informed a bemused audience: 'Unfortunately Mr Oscar Wilde is not in the house.' Even *Punch* grudgingly admitted that it was 'a work of some importance', and William Archer for *The World* wrote:

The one essential fact about Mr Oscar Wilde's dramatic work is that it must be taken on the very highest plane of modern English drama, and furthermore that it stands alone on that plane. In intellectual calibre, artistic competence – ay, and in dramatic instinct to boot, Mr Wilde has no rival among his fellow-workers for the stage. He is a thinker and a writer; they are more or less able, thoughtful, original playwrights ... he regards prose drama (so he has somewhere stated) as the lowest of the arts; and acting on this principle – the falsity of which he will discover as soon as a truly inspiring subject occurs to him – he amuses himself by lying on his back and blowing soap-bubbles for half an evening and then pretending, during the other half, to interest himself in some story of the simple affections such as audiences, he knows, regard as dramatic ... It is not his wit then, and still less his knack of paradox-twisting, that makes me claim for him a place apart among living English dramatists. It is the keen-ness of his intellect, the individuality of his point of view, the excellence of his verbal style and, above all, the genuinely dramatic quality of his inspirations.

Following this second great success, Oscar might have been expected to try for a third almost at once. Instead, the eighteen months which followed the first night of *A Woman of No Importance* were taken up in the pursuit of Bosie and the good life, both of which Oscar was now able to enjoy in the certain knowledge that his plays would pay for his excesses. That summer the Wildes took a cottage by the Thames at Goring, and Bosie, fresh from the scandal of being sent down from Oxford, joined them there. What Constance thought of the arrangement is not on record, but relations between her and Oscar were still good enough for her to be starting work on an anthology of his best lines, to be called *Oscariana*, and it seems likely that she and Bosie managed for a while to share Oscar's affections without too much domestic fury.

Since the Haymarket rehearsals, Max Beerbohm and his friend Reggie Turner had joined the ever-expanding Wilde/Douglas circle, a circle which included on its more respectable perimeter such Café Royal diners as Graham Robertson, Will Rothenstein, Aubrey Beardsley, Frank Harris, Bernard Shaw and A. E. W. Mason (for whom, in his struggling days, Oscar promised, 'there will always be lunch at the Café at one') and, on its darker edge, the renters who gathered around a male brothel then run over an empty Westminster bakery by Alfred Taylor, and whom he supplied virtually on order to Oscar and Bosie for the intimate suppers which Oscar later described in a letter as 'feasting with panthers'.

On the upper rim of the circle, it was Max Beerbohm who first noticed, and began to write about, the fact that Oscar really was going too far outside the acceptable moral and social conventions of the time. Asked to contribute some notes on Wilde to an Oxford magazine run by Alfred Douglas shortly before he was sent down, Max wrote: 'Luxury – gold-tipped matches – hair curled – Assyrian – wax statue – huge rings – fat white hands – not soigné – feather bed – pointed fingers – ample scarf – Louis Quinze cane – vast malmaison – cat-like tread – heavy shoulders – enormous dowager – or schoolboy – way of laughing with hand over mouth – stroking chin – looking up sideways – jollity overdone – But real vitality . . .' In one of his letters to Reggie Turner that summer, Max added: 'I am sorry to say that Oscar drinks far more than he ought . . . he has deteriorated very much in appear-ance – his cheeks being quite a dark purple and fat to a fault. I think he will die of apoplexy on the first night of a play.'

There is no doubt that Oscar's character was now undergoing a profound change. His two theatrical triumphs of the past fifteen months had merely confirmed his own opinion of his great talents but he really now believed himself above both criticism and the laws of Victorian society. The stories about him grew more and more exotic through the years 1893–4, not only sexually but also in his everyday behaviour. Sober observers like Conan Doyle thought he was going 'quite mad', and his devotion to the epigram at all costs was losing him not a few friendships, including that of the man about whom Oscar said: 'Poor fellow – he came to England to found a salon and succeeded only in opening a saloon.' This was a long-suffering if faintly sinister Russian émigré called André Raffalovich, to whom, for one Sunday lunch, Oscar was bidden in the company of Arthur Sullivan, George Grossmith, Allan Aynesworth, Arthur Cecil and Corney Grain. They were all gathered together on the doorstep as Raffalovich's butler answered the bell. 'Ah,' said Oscar, 'we'd like a table for six today, please.'

Two things of importance came to Oscar while he was staying in the cottage at Goring: the idea for *An Ideal Husband* and the first of a long series of letters from Ada Leverson, the writer who, known to Oscar always as 'The Sphinx', was to become the closest and most loyal of all his female friends. She wrote later:

Old legends heard in the schoolroom still hung like a mist over Oscar Wilde when I met him, and I was half surprised not to see him 'wan and palely loitering' in knee-breeches, holding the lily on the scent of which he had been said to subsist. But he had long given up the 'aesthetic' pose of the eighties [when] 'fired by the fervid words of the young Oscar, people threw their mahogany into the streets'.

But Oscar and Bosie were still quarrelling at Goring that summer ('Life in meadow and stream,' wrote Oscar from the cottage, 'is far more complex than is life in streets and salons') just as they had done in London and were to again at frequent intervals throughout a thoroughly stormy friendship. They made it up, however, and Oscar encouraged Bosie to do the English translation of his *Salomé* which was due to be published in an edition illustrated by Aubrey Beardsley. This in itself led to further quarrels: Oscar later told Bosie that his knowledge of French was 'unworthy of you as an ordinary Oxonian'. (Douglas's name never appeared on the title page of *Salomé*, and it is fair to assume that the translation was in the end partly Oscar's own, though in the book's dedication to Bosie he denies this.) There was a further quarrel with the publishers because some of Beardsley's drawings, notably those showing a depraved Herod looking eerily like Oscar himself, were thought indecent and had to be replaced.

By this time the Wilde/Douglas relationship had turned somewhat hysterical. After one particular Goring quarrel Wilde fled to Dinard and tried to end their friendship once and for all. Telegrams of fury, entreaty and remorse flew between the two men, and by November they were back together again, but by now, Oscar was worrying about Bosie's health. His own year had been almost totally occupied with the young Lord one way and another (his only publications of 1893 were two short prose poems and the script of *Lady Windermere's Fan*), and now he wrote to Lady Queensberry in some apparent anguish about her son:

> Bosie seems to me to be in a very bad state of health. He is sleepless, nervous, and rather hysterical. He seems to me quite altered. He is doing nothing in town . . . His life seems to me aimless, unhappy and absurd. All this is a great grief and disappointment to me, but he is very young, and terribly young in temperament. Why not try and make arrangements of some kind for him to go abroad for four or five months, to the Cromers in Egypt if that could be managed, where he would have new surroundings, proper friends and a different atmosphere? I think that if he stays in London he will not come to any good, and may spoil his young life irretrievably, quite irretrievably. Of course it will cost money no doubt, but here is the life of one of your sons – a life that should be brilliant and distinguished and charming – going quite astray, being quite ruined. I like to think myself his greatest friend – he, at any rate, makes me think so – so I write to you quite frankly to ask you to send him abroad to better surroundings. It would save him, I feel sure . . .

This of course could well have been a put-up job, and indeed parts of the letter read ominously as though dictated by Bosie. He after all welcomed the chance to travel, Egypt was well beyond Oscar's still shaky finances, and Wilde himself may have leapt at Bosie's suggestion that his mother should be encouraged to fork out the fare, on the grounds that it would give him some peace and quiet for the winter. At any event it worked.

As if to strengthen his case, Oscar also cabled (by now from 10 St James's Place, where he had rented rooms in order to work and maintain his own special kind of private life far away from the increasingly curious eyes of Constance and the boys) to More Adey, Robbie Ross's close friend: 'Bosie has influenza and is very pale.' But even while he was arranging for Bosie's departure there were other young men in the offing ('Lesley Thomson has appeared; he is extremely anxious to devote his whole life to me'), and within a few days Lady Queensberry, who knew all too well not only Oscar's proclivities but also Bosie's nature ('He is the one of my children who has inherited the fatal Douglas temperament'), found the money to send him off with the Cromers at a time when Lord Cromer was Consul General in Cairo.

Lady Cromer had been a childhood friend of Lady Queensberry, and their plan was that after a few months' embassy experience Bosie should be found a diplomatic posting elsewhere – one in Constantinople was subsequently offered, but declined. His mother begged Oscar not to follow Bosie to Cairo, and by now Wilde, as he later recalled in the letter to Bosie that was *De Profundis*, was again ready to end the affair once and for all: 'In the meantime you were writing to me by every post from Egypt. I took not the smallest notice of any of your communications.

I read them, and tore them up. I had quite settled to have no more to do with you. My mind was made up, and I gladly devoted myself to the Art whose progress I had allowed you to interrupt.'

In fact, Oscar was devoting himself to more than just Art: in the three months that Bosie spent in Cairo, visitors to his rooms in St James's Place included a large number of Alfred Taylor's young men, including Charlie Parker, Fred Atkins and Ernest Scarfe, to whom Oscar gave an inscribed silver cigarette case besides the inevitable private supper at the Café Royal or Kettner's. All these overnight visitors to St James's Place were unfortunately listed by a porter later to give evidence against Oscar, and it was already an open secret all over London that 'Hoskie's' tastes were getting rougher. The manager of at least one hotel much frequented in the past by Oscar, the Albemarle, now declined to have him or his young friends to stay overnight, and it is evident that Oscar was mistaken in his hope that the rooms in St James's would provide a much easier or more discreet rendezvous.

Meanwhile, in Cairo, Bosie was not behaving with any more tact or discretion than Oscar in London. He had met up with two young novelists, Robert Hichens and E. F. 'Dodo' Benson, with whom he sailed up the Nile when official embassy life with the Cromers grew too tedious to be endured. On that journey Bosie talked, indescribably indiscreetly, about himself and Oscar. Hichens, later to make his name as the author of *The Garden of Allah* and other bestsellers, was blessed with a retentive memory, and back in London during the following year he published a novel called *The Green Carnation*. Its central characters were Esmé Amarinth and Lord Reginald Hastings, and there could be no real doubt either about the identity of the two men on whom these characters were modelled or about the source of Hichens' information. It was not the first, nor the last, but it remains among the greatest of the many disservices done to Wilde by Alfred Douglas.

Yet their friendship (one is tempted to describe it as the original love-hate relationship) survived. 'My dearest Boy,' wrote Oscar to Bosie in Cairo, 'Thanks for your letter. I am overwhelmed by the wings of vulture creditors and out of sorts, but I am happy in the knowledge that we are friends again, and that our love has passed through the shadow and the night of estrangement and sorrow and come out rose-crowned as of old. Let us always be infinitely dear to each other, as indeed we have been always.'

And it was in this reconciliatory mood that the two men agreed to meet in Paris on Bosie's way back to England. In *De Profundis*, Oscar recalled for Bosie the reasons for this:

You arrived in Paris late on a Saturday night, and found a brief letter from me waiting at your hotel stating that I would not see you. Next morning I received in Tite Street a telegram of some ten or eleven pages in length from you. You stated in it that no matter what you had done to me you could not believe that I would absolutely decline to see you; you reminded me that for the sake of seeing me even for one hour you had travelled six days and nights across Europe without stopping once on the way; you made what I must admit was a most pathetic appeal, and ended with what seemed to me a threat of suicide, and one not thinly veiled. You had yourself often told me how many of your race there had been who had stained their hands in their own blood; your uncle, certainly, your grandfather, possibly; and many others in the mad, bad line from which you are come. Pity, my old affection for you ... mere humanity itself – all these, if excuses be necessary, must serve as my excuse for consenting to accord you one last interview. When I arrived in Paris, your tears, breaking out again and again all through the evening, and falling over your cheeks like rain as we sat, at dinner first at Voisin's, at supper at Paillard's afterwards; the unfeigned joy you evinced at seeing me, holding my hand whenever you could, as though you were a gentle and penitent child; your contrition, so simple and sincere, at the moment: made me consent to renew our friendship. Two days after we had returned to London, your father saw you having luncheon with me at the Café Royal, joined my table, drank of my wine, and that afternoon, through a letter addressed to you, began his first attack on me.

The 'attack' of the Marquis of Queensberry had been coming for some weeks. By now, with the publication of *The Green Carnation*, all fashionable London was talking about the Wilde/Douglas friendship: they themselves had, after all, scarcely been at pains to conceal it and the stories surrounding their affairs with each other and with Taylor's renters grew daily more fanciful. Nor was Robbie Ross able to remain totally aloof, as a letter from Max Beerbohm to Reggie Turner in December 1893 indicates:

Bobbie Ross has returned to this country for a few days and of him there have been very great and intimate scandals and almost, if not quite, warrants. Slowly he is recovering but has to remain at Davos during his convalescence for fear of a social relapse. I must not disclose anything (nor must you), but I may tell you that a schoolboy with wonderful eyes, Bosie, Robbie, a furious father, George Lewis, a headmaster (who is now blackmailing Robbie), St John Wontner, Calais, Dover, Oscar Browning, Oscar, Dover, Calais, intercepted letters, private detectives, Calais, Dover and returned cigarette-cases were some of the ingredients of the dreadful episode ... the 'garçon entretenu' was the same as him of whom I told you that he had been stolen from Bobbie by Bosie and kept at Albemarle Hotel ...

Such gossip was also reaching the ears of the Marquis and, to say the least, he did not care for it. The idea that a son of his, a member of the most ancient noble family of Scotland, should be involved in an apparently homosexual affair, and with a playwright, was more than flesh or blood could stand – especially where the blood boiled as speedily as that of the 'mad Marquis'. What worried him initially, though, was not the truth of the rumours – since he admitted to being in some doubt about whether Oscar and Bosie were actually sleeping together – but their very existence. He wrote to his son after that fateful Café Royal encounter:

Your intimacy with this man Wilde must either cease or I will disown you and stop all money supplies. I am not going to try and analyse this intimacy, and I make no charge; but to my mind to pose as a thing is as bad as to be it. With my own eyes I saw you both in the most loathsome and disgusting relationship as expressed by your manner and expression. Never in my experience have I ever seen such a sight as that in your horrible features. No wonder people are talking as they are. Also I now hear on good authority, but this may be false [it was] that his wife is petitioning to divorce him for sodomy and other crimes. Is this true, or do you not know of it? I thought if the actual thing was true, and it became public property, I should be quite justified in shooting him at sight. These Christian English cowards and men, as they call themselves, want waking up . . .

In reply, Bosie merely telegraphed: 'What a funny little man you are,' thereby ensuring, as he well knew, that his father's already dangerously high temper would be lost forever. The Marquis stormed back:

You impertinent young jackanapes, I request that you will not send such messages to me by telegraph. If you send me any more such telegrams, or come with any impertinence, I will give you the thrashing you deserve. Your only excuse is that you must be crazy. I hear from a man at Oxford that you were thought crazy there, and that accounts for a good deal that has happened. If I catch you again with that man I will make a public scandal in a way you little dream of; if it is already a suppressed one, I prefer an open one, and at any rate I shall not be blamed for allowing such a state of things to go on. Unless this acquaintance ceases I shall carry out my threat and stop all supplies, and if you are not going to make any attempt to do something I shall certainly cut you down to a mere pittance, so you know what to expect.

At first neither Oscar nor Bosie saw anything very serious to worry about. After all, Oscar had known of the Marquis's existence for some time (he had even invited him to stay with Constance and the children and Bosie and himself at Babbacombe, an invitation Lord Queensberry unsurprisingly had declined), and six months before that terrible burst of correspondence about Oscar between father and son, the three of them had met for lunch at the Café Royal. At the end of their meal Bosie had left the two older men together, and Queensberry had by all accounts been totally won over by the legendary Wildean charm.

Now, however, things were different, and the Marquis was very irate indeed. At the end of June 1894 he even called on Oscar at Tite Street, and the following is Oscar's own account of that occasion:

The interview took place in my library. Lord Queensberry was standing by the window, I walked over to the fireplace, and he said to me 'Sit down'. I said to him 'I do not allow any one to talk like that to me in my own house or anywhere else. I suppose you have come to apologize for the statement you made about my wife and myself in letters you wrote to your son. I should have the right any day I chose to prosecute you for writing such a letter.' He said 'The letter was privileged, as it was

written to my son.' I said 'How dare you say such things to me about your son and me?'
He said 'You were both kicked out of the Savoy Hotel at a moment's notice for your
disgusting conduct.' I said 'That is a lie' ... He said 'I hear you were thoroughly
blackmailed for a disgusting letter you wrote to my son.' I said 'That letter was a
beautiful letter and I never write anything except for publication.' Then I asked 'Lord
Queensberry, do you seriously accuse your son and me of improper conduct?' He said
'I do not say you are it, but you look it, and you pose as it, which is just as bad. If I
catch you and my son together in any public restaurant I will thrash you.' I said 'I do
not know what the Queensberry rules are, but the Oscar Wilde rule is to shoot at sight.'
I then told Lord Queensberry to leave my house. He said he would not do so ... I
then went into the hall and pointed him out to my servant. I said 'This is the Marquis
of Queensberry, the most infamous brute in London. You are never to allow him to
enter my house again.'

Lady Queensberry, meanwhile, equally determined to separate her son from the
dread Oscar, had sent Bosie to Florence. There however he was soon joined not only
by Oscar but also by André Gide, a twosome not exactly guaranteed to keep Bosie
on the paths of heterosexual virtue. Douglas, though now all of twenty-five, still
looked like a teenager, and although a fair number of otherwise intelligent people
(among them Frank Harris and Bernard Shaw) were still convinced there was
nothing in the least untoward about the young man's friendship with Wilde, the
Marquis himself entertained little doubt. 'Your father is on the rampage again,'
wrote Oscar to Bosie in August 1894, 'has been to the Café Royal to enquire for us
with threats etc. I think now it would have been better for me to have had him
bound over to keep the peace, ,but what a scandal! Still, it is intolerable to be
dogged by a maniac.'

Besides, all this was leaving Oscar precious little time to concentrate on his
writing, and although 1894 was to be the year in which he finished both *An Ideal
Husband* and *The Importance of Being Earnest* there was nothing else to show for it
beyond some more short prose poems and one in verse called 'The Sphinx', which
he had been working on intermittently ever since the contract for it with John
Lane had been signed two summers back. *Punch* inevitably came up with a parody
of it, but a gentle one this time, written by Oscar's new friend the 'Sphinx' herself,
Ada Leverson, but beyond that it provoked little real interest. By now the first
issue of *The Yellow Book* (with Beardsley as art editor) was on the streets, and
'The Sphinx' seemed more than a little passé. But Oscar was not above writing
for other magazines still, though he left *The Yellow Book* well alone, and when in
the autumn of 1894 Frank Harris took over the *Saturday Review* Wilde cheerfully
cobbled together nineteen 'Maxims for the Instruction of the Over-Educated':

Education is an admirable thing. But it is well to remember from time to time that
nothing that is worth knowing can be taught.

Public opinion exists only where there are no ideas.

Salomé *was written in 1892 but refused a stage licence for several years thereafter;* (top left) *Maud Allen in a 1908 production.*
Top right *Nazimova in the 1922 film of* Salomé *designed by Natasha Rambova.*
Above *The opera* Salomé, *first staged in Dresden in 1905.*

A playwright of some importance.

Oscar in Paris (centre left) *visualized by Toulouse-Lautrec, 1895.*

The Importance of Being Earnest: *George Alexander as John Worthing in the first production, 1895.*

Below *The castlist of the first production.*

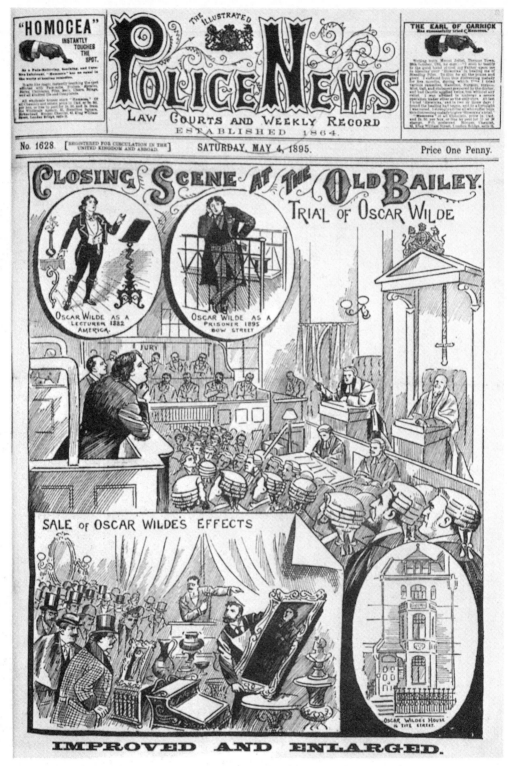

*The rise and fall of Oscar Wilde, told in pictures
on the cover of* The Police News.

Left *Oscar released and in Rome, April 1900. 'I have not seen the Holy Father since last Thursday but am bearing up wonderfully well.'*
Top right *The Hôtel de la Plage at Berneval, Oscar's home for the summer of 1897.*
Right *Wilde's tomb, designed by Epstein, at Père Lachaise in Paris.*

Ernst Lubitsch (left) directing May McAvoy and Ronald Colman in the 1925 silent film version of Lady Windermere's Fan.

Bernard Aldor in a German film version of The Picture of Dorian Gray.

Top left *A poster for the Paris stage production of* Oscar Wilde *by Leslie and Sewell Stokes.*
Top *Robert Morley in the London Gate Theatre club production of the Stokes'* Oscar Wilde,
September 1936.
Top right *Micheál Liammóir in* The Importance of Being Oscar.
Centre and above *Robert Morley and Peter Finch in two separate film biographies of Wilde
simultaneously released in 1960.*

Stephen Fry as Oscar Wilde, by Lord Snowdon

The English are always degrading truths into facts. When a truth becomes a fact it loses all its intellectual value.

It is a very sad thing that nowadays there is so little useless information.

The only link between Literature and the Drama left to us in England at the present moment is the bill of the play.

In old days books were written by men of letters and read by the public. Nowadays books are written by the public and read by nobody.

Most women are so artificial that they have no sense of Art. Most men are so natural that they have no sense of Beauty.

Friendship is far more tragic than love. It lasts longer.

What is abnormal in Life stands in normal relation to Art. It is the only thing in Life that stands in normal relation to Art.

A subject that is beautiful in itself gives no suggestion to the artist. It lacks imperfection.

The only thing that the artist cannot see is the obvious. The only thing that the public can see is the obvious. The result is the Criticism of the journalist.

Art is the only serious thing in the world. And the artist is the only person who is never serious.

To be really mediaeval one should have no body. To be really modern one should have no soul. To be really Greek one should have no clothes.

Dandyism is the assertion of the absolute modernity of Beauty.

The only thing that can console one for being poor is extravagance. The only thing that can console one for being rich is economy.

One should never listen. To listen is a sign of indifference to one's hearers.

Even the disciple has his uses. He stands behind one's throne, and at the moment of one's triumph whispers in one's ear that, after all, one is immortal.

The criminal classes are so close to us that even the policeman can see them. They are so far away from us that only the poet can understand them.

Those whom the gods love grow young.

But Oscar's primary professional interest was still in the theatre – indeed versions of those Maxims in dialogue form can be found in each and every one of his four major comedies – and early in 1894 (feeling no particular sense of loyalty to either of his first two producers, Alexander and Tree) he approached yet another actor-manager of the period, Lewis Waller, with the idea that he should undertake a Wilde triple bill, to consist of one new play (*An Ideal Husband*) plus the two earlier comedies in revival. Waller declined, though he was within a year to produce and appear in *An Ideal Husband* after this had been on a round of other managers' offices without success.

Wilde was much in evidence around London's West End at this time, whether going backstage at the St James's to introduce Aubrey Beardsley to Mrs Patrick Campbell, or simply making fun of the Trees, who were then appearing in a children's play called *Once Upon A Time*. ('Since the appearance of Tree in his pyjamas,' wrote Oscar to Mrs Bernard Beere, 'there has been the greatest sympathy for Mrs Tree. It throws a lurid light on the difficulties of their married life.') But it was now a year since the London opening of *A Woman of No Importance*, and the touring productions of his first two comedies had also closed, leaving Oscar yet again in dire financial straits. There was also now a certain amount of trouble with the tradesmen, notably a shopkeeper who kept him supplied with cigarettes for Alfred Douglas. In the summer, Oscar wrote to Bosie:

Dearest Boy, I hope to send you the cigarettes, if Simmonds will let me have them. He has applied for his bill. I am overdrawn £41 at the bank; it really is intolerable the want of money. I have not a penny. I can't stand it any longer, but don't know what to do. I go down to Worthing tomorrow. I hope to do work there. The house, I hear, is very small, and I have no writing room. However, anything is better than London.

It was at Worthing, towards the end of summer 1894, that Oscar at last found the time and the comparative tranquillity ('A horrid ugly Swiss governess has I find been looking after Cyril and Vyvyan for a year. She is quite impossible. Also, children at meals are tedious') to start work on the last and greatest of his four comedies. As was by now his custom, he named the leading character after the place where he was conceived, and thus John Worthing and *The Importance of Being Earnest* were born.

Back in London, meanwhile, the panthers were under attack; on 12 August the police raided a club at 46 Fitzroy Street and arrested eighteen men, 'two of them in female dress'. Alfred Taylor was among the eighteen, and in reply to a demand for money from his friend Charles Mason, Oscar wrote: 'It is a dreadful piece of bad luck and I wish to goodness I could do something for him, but, as I have had occasion to write to him many times lately, as I have no play going on this season I have no money at all and indeed am at my wits' end trying to raise some for household expenses and such tedious things . . .'

Taylor was however acquitted on this occasion, and Oscar seems still not to have had the remotest notion of the danger in which he remained. His letters to and about Alfred Taylor indicate that he still thought himself untouchable by either police or public opinion concerning his private life, and that belief still had the best part of nine months to run. In the meantime he occupied himself by extracting an advance from George Alexander for *The Importance* . . . (at present called *Lady Lancing*), and adding some 'improvements' to Constance's collection of 'Oscariana'. He also kept in touch with his old Parisian friend Robert Sherard, though their relationship was somewhat strained by Sherard's request that Oscar

should give an interview to an American journalist friend of his. 'If,' replied
Oscar, 'McClure wishes me to be interviewed he must pay me . . . the classical sum
is I believe £20. Of course he won't do this: why on earth should he? But I certainly
won't give him a column of conversation to amuse his readers for nothing. Besides,
I'm sick of my name in the papers.'

From Worthing (and possibly to escape Constance, the children, the ugly Swiss
governess and all the trappings of a middle-class English seaside holiday) Oscar
took Bosie along the coast to Brighton, where they nursed each other increasingly
acrimoniously through bouts of influenza before returning to London. There the
interest aroused by Taylor's arrest seemed to have died away, and Oscar set about
casting and other preparations for both *An Ideal Husband* and *The Importance of
Being Earnest*, tasks which took him through to Christmas. Queensberry seems to
have been lying remarkably low in these months, possibly because he believed that
his irate visit to Tite Street had discouraged Oscar's friendship with his son, or,
more probably, because he was himself by now deeply involved in the turmoil of
his second marriage and divorce.

Others, though, were now beginning to write more openly of Oscar's private
life – among them Max Beerbohm, in a remarkably indiscreet piece conceived for,
but never published in, the first issue of *The Yellow Book*. Called 'A Peep into the
Past', this was a joky account of Oscar living 'a life of quiet retirement in his little
house in Tite Street' and it included such heavy-handed hints as: 'Himself most
regular in his habits, he is something of a martinet about punctuality in his household and perhaps this accounts for the constant succession of page-boys which so
startles the neighbourhood.'

By now, Oscar had in fact again decided to break with Bosie once and for all.
Douglas was proving (not for the first time) a less than reliable friend, actually
arriving at Worthing station with a younger lover in tow on one occasion, and on
another abandoning Oscar in the final throes of his influenza at Brighton. 'When
you are not on your pedestal,' wrote Bosie by way of later explanation, 'you are
not interesting. The next time you are ill I will go away at once.' Oscar, deciding
that this time Bosie had gone too far, arranged to have his solicitor (now Sir)
George Lewis tell Queensberry that Oscar intended never again to see his son. At
that precise moment, however, Bosie's elder brother was found shot through the
head in what looked much like suicide. Oscar cabled Bosie his condolences, and
the whole ill-fated friendship started afresh.

10
TWO TRIUMPHS...
AND THREE TRIALS

—

1895

1895, the best and the worst year in Oscar's life, started well enough: with Tree away on tour in America, Lewis Waller had agreed to take *An Ideal Husband* into the Haymarket and Alexander was preparing *The Importance of Being Earnest* for the St James's. Waller opened first: *An Ideal Husband* had its première on 3 January, with a cast headed by himself, Charles Hawtrey and Julia Neilson, and with Charles Brookfield in the comparatively minor role of the Valet. It was Brookfield who had co-written the parody, 'The Poet and the Puppets' a couple of years earlier; supposed by some to be an illegitimate son of Thackeray, he was an interesting figure of the London theatrical scene, whom many later suspected to be among the most active in gathering evidence against Wilde, by whom he apparently believed himself to have been snubbed.

But that was still to come. The opening of *An Ideal Husband* was an unqualified success, with the Prince of Wales himself in the royal box. Bernard Shaw, who had just become drama critic of Harris's *Saturday Review*, was ecstatic ('In a certain sense Mr Wilde is to me our only thorough playwright. He plays with everything: with wit, with philosophy, with drama, with actors and audience, with the whole theatre. Such a feat scandalizes the Englishman, who can no more play with wit and philosophy than he can with a football or a cricket bat') and even *Punch* grudgingly allowed that it was 'an interesting play up to the end of the Third Act'. In fact, *An Ideal Husband* is the most thoughtful of all Wilde's comedies, concerned as it is with the attempted blackmailing of Sir Robert Chiltern (Waller) by the redoubtable Mrs Cheveley (Florence West), a plot which suggests that the attempted blackmail of Wilde a few months earlier had not been entirely fruitless.

The Prince of Wales enjoyed it hugely, and advised Wilde to cut 'not a word of it'. Henry James was altogether less enthusiastic: attending a performance while his own *Guy Domville* was in preparation, he found it 'crude, clumsy, feeble and vulgar', and decided that his own play could not possibly succeed if London audiences were stupid enough to enjoy this one – a prophetic belief, since *Guy Domville* was to be replaced at the St James's within a month or two by *The Importance of Being Earnest*, thereby increasing James's dislike of Oscar a hundredfold. Wilde himself said that *An Ideal Husband* contained 'a great deal of the real Oscar', and Max Beerbohm reckoned that it was 'stagey' but had to admit that it worked.

Although *An Ideal Husband* proved in the end to be the least commercially successful of all the four major plays (and remains the least often revived), the early box-office takings were healthy enough to allow Oscar and Bosie to take off for a holiday in Algiers within a fortnight of the first performance. There, almost a year after their brief encounter in Florence, the two men again met André Gide, who later recalled:

Wilde had certainly changed. One felt less softness in his look, something raucous in his laughter and something frenzied in his joy. He seemed both more sure of pleasing and less ambitious to succeed in doing so; he was bolder, stronger, bigger . . . He would walk in the streets of Algiers, preceded, escorted, followed by an extraordinary band of ragamuffins; he chatted with each one; he regarded them all with joy and tossed his money to them haphazardly. 'I hope,' he said to me, 'to have quite demoralized this city.'

The fortnight that Wilde and Bosie and Gide spent pursuing Arab boys around Algiers was unarguably the last totally free and happy period of Oscar's life. The call of duty in the form of rehearsals for *The Importance* . . . grew too loud however, even for so practised a resister, and Oscar left Gide and Bosie in Algiers – Bosie to pursue a boy to Biskra and Gide following them to see what would happen; what did was that the boy deserted Bosie for a girl and the latter returned somewhat disconsolately to London in time for the first night of *The Importance of Being Earnest*.

By now, though, his father was back in action. Hearing of Bosie's journey to Algiers in the company of the infamous Wilde (but not, presumably, of the way it ended), in direct contravention of his paternal instructions of the previous year, Queensberry let it be known that he planned to attend the opening night and to make his presence felt there. George Alexander, hearing of this from Lady Queensberry, had the booking cancelled, just one of the services he performed for Oscar during a somewhat fraught rehearsal period.

Oscar had returned from Algiers in full flood, only too eager to give Alexander a series of production notes after every run-through. Relations between the two men were already rather strained: Wilde had originally sent his comedy to Charles Wyndham, on the grounds that Alexander was 'too romantic' a player to do it any good. Wyndham had then found himself in a long-running success, and in no hurry to produce the play, so he had assigned it to Alexander, who pulled the script back from four acts to three and cast himself, Allan Aynesworth, Irene Vanburgh and Mrs Edward Saker (Rose Leclercq) in the four principal roles.

Wilde's interruptions at rehearsal finally grew too frequent for Alexander to bear, and he was barred from the theatre: not, however, before he had summoned Alexander and Aynesworth to meet him for dinner at his club, the Albemarle. There the two actors arrived, tired and more than a little nervous, to be met in the door-way by Oscar. 'My dear Aleck,' he said, 'and my dear Aynesworth, I have only one thing to say to you. You are neither of you my favourite actor. We will now go in to supper.' Having thus made his point, Oscar left Alexander and his company alone for the last few days of their rehearsals. Asked at this time by a reporter if he thought the play would be a success, he replied: 'It already is: the only question is whether the first-night audience will be one too.'

They arrived, that first-night audience, in a raging blizzard. The night of 14 February 1895 saw the worst snowstorm London had experienced for several years; through it tramped, among others, the Marquis of Queensberry, ac-companied by his faithful bruiser. Denied admission at the front doors of the St James's, they went round the side, trying to get in at first the gallery and then the stage door with a bizarre bouquet of carrots and turnips which the Marquis in his continuing frenzy apparently intended to hurl at Oscar as he took his author's curtain call.

Queensberry failed to get in, however, and in any case Oscar had no intention of appearing on the stage that night. He had, he explained to Aynesworth back-stage during the show, only recently taken a call from the stage at the opening of *An Ideal Husband*, and to go on doing so at frequent intervals would make him feel like a German band. There was a tumultuous reception as the curtain fell, and after hearing the applause Wilde climbed the stairs to Alexander's dressing room. 'Well?' asked the actor-manager. 'Charming,' replied Oscar, 'quite charming. And do you know, from time to time it reminded me of a play I once wrote myself, called *The Importance of Being Earnest*.'

But next morning the critics were in no doubt about where to assign the credit. William Archer for *The World* reckoned that Wilde had sent 'wave after wave of laughter curling and foaming round the theatre', though he added of the play: 'It is like a mirage-oasis in the desert, grateful and comforting to the weary eye – but when you come up close to it, behold! it is intangible, it eludes your grasp,' thereby putting into print overnight the problem that was to face critics for the next three-quarters of a century. For *The Importance of Being Earnest* remains an elusive triumph: though it has been revived more often than the rest of Wilde's plays put together, though it is generally reckoned to be the finest 'modern' comedy in the English language, and though it has been translated into almost every other, it resists description. Loosely concerned with John Worthing's search for his own identity, one that was once mislaid along with himself in a handbag at Victoria Station, it is in reality a series of brilliant confidence tricks played by the characters on each other and their audience. H. G. Wells, writing in the *Pall Mall Gazette*, thought it 'all very funny', though Bernard Shaw, hitherto an avowed Wilde fan, noted: 'It amused me, of course, but unless comedy touches me as well as amuses me it leaves me with a sense of having wasted my evening.'

Others in later years were to express other doubts: the American critic Mary McCarthy, for instance, writing in her 1963 'Theatre Chronicles':

Written on the brink of his fall, *The Importance of Being Earnest* is Wilde's true *De Profundis*; the other was false sentiment. This is hell, and if a great deal of it is tiresome, eternity is, as M. Sartre says, a bore. The tone of the Wilde dialogue, inappropriate to the problem drama, perfectly reflects the conditions in this infernal Arcadia: peevish, fretful, valetudinarian, it is the tone of an elderly recluse who lives imprisoned by his comforts; it combines the finicky and the greedy, like a piggish old lady.

But talking of piggish old ladies there is, as Miss McCarthy grudgingly acknowledges, the all-saving presence of Lady Bracknell, a character who transcends in her rumbling fury all the rest of Wilde's dramatic creations. She it is who, told of John Worthing's unfortunate loss of both parents replies: 'To lose one parent may be regarded as a misfortune . . . to lose both seems like carelessness.' She it is who, told how the infant Worthing was found at Victoria in a handbag, replies: 'To be born or at any rate bred in a handbag, whether it had handles or not, seems to me to display a contempt for the ordinary decencies of family life that reminds one of the worst excesses of the French Revolution. And I presume you know what that unfortunate movement led to?' And she it is who, told of Worthing's lack of education, replies: 'I am pleased to hear it. I do not approve of anything that tampers with natural ignorance. Ignorance is like a delicate exotic fruit; touch it and the bloom is gone. The whole theory of modern education is radically unsound. Fortunately in England, at any rate, education produces no effect whatsoever. If it did, it would prove a serious danger to the upper classes, and probably lead to acts of violence in Grosvenor Square.'

There is, in short, no one in the whole of English dramatic literature quite like Lady Bracknell. Equally there is no play quite like *The Importance of Being Earnest* which perhaps explains why, seventy-five years after its original creation, such diverse playwrights as Tom Stoppard and Alan Bennett could parody it in their own work, totally secure in the knowledge that its landmarks would be recognized by all.

Still, Shaw did not care for it. Wilde himself called the play 'a trivial comedy for serious people', but G.B.S. had more serious reservations:

Clever as it was, it was his first really heartless play. In the others, the chivalry of the eighteenth-century Irishman and the romance of the disciple of Théophile Gautier (Oscar was really old-fashioned in the Irish way, except as a critic of morals) not only gave a certain kindness and gallantry to the serious passages and to the handling of the women, but provided that proximity of emotion without which laughter, however irresistible, is destructive and sinister. In *The Importance of Being Earnest* this had vanished and the play, though extremely funny, was essentially hateful. I had no idea that Oscar was going to the dogs, and that this represented a real degeneracy produced by his debaucheries. I thought he was still developing: and I hazarded the unhappy guess that *The Importance of Being Earnest* was in idea a young work written or projected long before, under the influence of Gilbert, and furbished up for Alexander as a potboiler. At the Café Royal I calmly asked him whether I was not right. He indignantly repudiated my guess and said loftily . . . that he was disappointed in me.

Wilde could afford to be disappointed with one lone dissenter: he now had the two most successful comedies on the London stage running simultaneously above his name at the Haymarket and the St James's, and there seemed for a brief moment no reason why they should not both run profitably on through to the end of the 1894–5 season.

With the proceeds, Oscar and Bosie managed to pay off some of their debts at the Avondale Hotel in Piccadilly where the manager later insisted on impounding the luggage until they could clear the rest. Unperturbed, Oscar continued to celebrate the triumph of a play which, as A. B. Walkley in the *Spectator* said, established him as the 'master creator of sheer nonsense'. Wilde himself joined in the praise: 'The first act is ingenious, the second beautiful and the third abominably clever.' That there had also once been a fourth (cut by Alexander), in which Worthing found himself in imminent danger of imprisonment for unpaid debts, may lend credence to the theory that there is also more of Oscar in *The Importance of Being Earnest* than he would have admitted. A play, after all, about a man able to lead a double life, changing his name at will and disappearing for illicit weekends of 'Bunburying', had certain echoes of his own private life – a life about to be made gruesomely public.

The Marquis of Queensberry returned to his home after his failure to deliver the vegetable bouquet on the first night, and an already raging temper was not calmed by the glowing Press notices for Wilde in his papers the following morning. It took him three full days to decide what to do next, and in the meantime Oscar had been told about his appearance at the theatre. He wrote to Bosie on 17 February:

Dearest Boy, yes; the Scarlet Marquis made a plot to address the audience on the first night of my play! Algy Bourke revealed it, and he was not allowed to enter. He left a grotesque bouquet of vegetables for me! This of course makes his conduct idiotic, robs it of dignity. He arrived with a prize-fighter! I had all Scotland Yard –

twenty police – to guard the theatre. He prowled about for three hours, then left chattering like a monstrous ape.

'I feel now,' Oscar added, 'that without your name being mentioned all will go well.' Evidently he believed that Queensberry's thwarted gesture of defiance would be the end of his protests, and that he was now in any case protected by his own success.

Sadly, he was not. On the following day (18 February) Queensberry took himself to Wilde's club, the Albemarle, and there left with the hall porter a visiting card on the back of which he had spelt out (or rather misspelt out): 'To Oscar Wilde, posing as somdomite.'

The hall porter tactfully placed the card in a sealed envelope, and there it sat, like a time bomb, awaiting Oscar's next visit to the club, which as chance would have it was not for another ten days. In the meantime, spurred on by his double triumph in the West End and by the realization that he might at last be able to pay off his debts ('I am already served with writs for £400, rumours of my prosperity having reached the commercial classes'), he was already writing to Alexander about *A Florentine Tragedy*, which he had started writing in the previous year but was never to finish.

He was also writing to his beloved Ada Leverson, congratulating her on the now ritualistic *Punch* parody she had written (entitled 'The Advisability Of Not Being Brought Up In A Handbag: A Trivial Tragedy For Wonderful People'), and was in generally celebratory mood:

The gods had given me almost everything. I had genius, a distinguished name, high social position, brilliancy, intellectual daring: I made art a philosophy and philosophy an art: I altered the minds of men and the colours of things; there was nothing I said or did that did not make people wonder ... drama, novel, poem in rhyme, poem in prose, subtle or fantastic dialogue, whatever I touched I made beautiful in a new mode of beauty; to truth itself I gave what is false no less than what is true as its rightful province, and showed that the false and true are merely forms of intellectual existence. I treated Art as the supreme reality, and life as a mere mode of fiction; I awoke the imagination of my century so that it created myth and legend around me: I summed up all systems in a phrase, and all existence in an epigram.

A number of critics, Shaw among them, noted later that Wilde's subsequent fall had a kind of inevitability about it, since his own high opinion of himself, coupled with his affectations of speech and dress, had effectively cut him off from contact with the kind of 'real people' who could lead him back towards the straight and narrow. Yet that was the wisdom of hindsight; for now, it appeared that Oscar could still do no wrong, or at least none that could not be overlooked by an indulgent group of friends and admirers. Two such were Charles Ricketts and C. H. Shannon, the young illustrators whom Wilde had befriended when they worked with him (Ricketts on *Dorian Gray* and the poems, Shannon on the published text of *Lady Windermere's Fan*), and for whom he was ever to retain a certain wary affection. Told by Rothenstein when almost on his deathbed that they had at last found real commercial success, Wilde murmured: 'Ah, I suppose when you go there to supper now they give you *fresh* eggs.'

Wilde called to see the two men on 28 February. Shannon was out, but Ricketts spent some time discussing his plans to republish 'The Portrait of Mr W. H.'. Wilde then left for his club where, at last, he found the 'somdomite' card left by the Marquis more than a week earlier. The hall porter assured Oscar that he had placed it immediately in an envelope, and that it had therefore been seen by nobody except himself, and he had not understood it.

Oscar, in high agitation, returned to the Avondale and from there sent an immediate note – not, interestingly enough, to Alfred Douglas, but instead to an older and more reliable friend, one who was now to reclaim his place in the forefront of the Wilde story, Robbie Ross:

Dearest Bobbie: Since I saw you something has happened. Bosie's father has left a card at my club with hideous words on it. I don't see anything now but a criminal prosecution. My whole life seems ruined by this man. The tower of ivory is assailed by the foul thing. On the sand is my life spilt. I don't know what to do. If you could come here at 11.30 please do so tonight. I mar your life by trespassing ever on your love and kindness. I have asked Bosie to come tomorrow . . .

Robbie hastened round from his room in Hornton Street, only to find Bosie already arrived by chance at Oscar's hotel. Together they decided that there was indeed only one thing to do. Oscar should apply for a warrant charging the Marquis of Queensberry with criminal libel.

It is at this point that views of Wilde's subsequent behaviour diverge most abruptly. The conventional wisdom is that he did a rash and foolish thing, spurred only by Alfred Douglas's hatred of his father, and that the events of the next three months, culminating in Oscar's prison sentence, could have been neatly and totally sidestepped had Oscar simply torn up the card that night at the Albemarle. It is an attractive theory, but depends on the extent to which you believe in Bosie's stranglehold on Oscar and are prepared to ignore the wording of Oscar's first letter to Robbie Ross.

Wilde was now at the height of his fame and power; his friendship with Alfred Douglas, though intermittently passionate, had been frequently interrupted by affairs with other boys (as late as 10 February 1895 he was writing to Ada Leverson asking if he might bring to dinner 'a young man tall as a palm tree . . . his christian name is Tom'), and it seems difficult therefore to believe that he was so totally and utterly obsessed with Douglas that he was prepared to risk open court simply and solely to satisfy Bosie's craving for a fight with his father. If this was so, moreover, how to explain Oscar's letter to Robbie in which, before Bosie has even arrived for consultation, he is so determined to sue?

But why else issue the writ? There is no evidence that Robbie Ross opposed the decision, and it seems likely that Wilde would have listened more carefully to his comparatively detached advice than to that of Bosie. It may therefore have appeared to Ross, and then also to Oscar once Ross had explained it, that the Marquis having gone so far would doubtless go further unless forcibly restrained. The unsuccessful delivery of the bouquet, followed by the successful delivery of the card, might yet be followed by a third and more violent approach of some kind, and there must eventually be a limit, no matter how hazy, to the amount of pressure of this kind Oscar's cherished public image could stand.

Moreover, a writ for libel must have seemed a temptingly simple pre-emptive strike. Queensberry was unlikely to have (indeed did not then have) any evidence beyond the letters from Oscar to Bosie, and he had already played that hand unsuccessfully during the meeting at Tite Street. It must thus have appeared, in that situation, no great problem to have the mad Marquis legally silenced once and for all – since that would surely be the outcome of such a trial. To this argument, it may be assumed, Bosie would have lent eager support rather than a driving urge, and although the outcome remained the same needless catastrophe, the blame for it cannot be laid at his door alone.

Other mistakes followed in rapid succession: the morning after their meeting at the Avondale, Oscar went to consult not Sir George Lewis, a lawyer by now well versed in problems arising from the law's attitude to homosexuality (and later to be retained albeit briefly by Queensberry), but instead Robbie Ross's solicitor, Charles Humphreys, a man so unversed in the ways of Oscar's world that he first of all asked if there was any truth in the libel. Wilde promised him that there was not, a promise apparently made in the presence of Ross and Douglas, neither of whom thought to deny it nor to alert Oscar to the danger he faced if by any chance the lie could be disproved in court. On the following morning, 2 March, the Marquis was taken from his room at Carter's Hotel to Vine Street police station, where he was charged with criminal libel. From there he was taken before the magistrate at Great Marlborough Street, who remanded him on bail for a week. The machinery had thus been set in full motion.

During the next seven days Oscar was frantically searching around for money to cover his legal expenses. Bosie's family, all eager to see the Marquis in trouble, came up with £360, and the faithful Ada Leverson's husband stumped up another £500 which Oscar thought would be needed in advance. Bosie's elder brother, son and heir to the Marquis, had promised to pay one half of the eventual costs.

Everything therefore seemed under control and there was even good news from 'the Sibyl Robinson', a fortune-teller by whom Oscar set great store, and who now prophesied complete triumph, despite the fact that she had earlier told Oscar that she foresaw a brilliant life for him 'up to a certain point. Then I see a wall. Beyond the wall I see nothing.'

During this week, each side instructed counsel. Queensberry retained Edward Carson, who had been at Trinity College, Dublin, with Wilde ('No doubt,' said Oscar 'he will perform his task with the added bitterness of an old friend'). On Wilde's behalf, Humphreys retained Sir Edward Clarke, then Solicitor-General and a man with a victorious reputation. He too questioned Wilde, and he too was assured that there was no vestige of truth in the allegation of sodomy.

On 9 March, Wilde, Bosie and his elder brother all appeared at Great Marlborough Street. The magistrate directed Lord Alfred to leave at once (since he was the source of contention between the litigants), and as the Defence had at this stage nothing to offer except certain dubious passages quoted from *Dorian Gray*, and the old letters, Queensberry was duly committed for trial, his bail now set at £500. There was also, at these preliminary proceedings, a nutshell indication of how the actual trial would go. Asked by the magistrate if he was by profession a dramatist and author, Oscar replied: 'I believe that I am well known in that capacity.' 'Only answer the questions, please,' snapped the magistrate. Queensberry, on the other hand, managed to make a far better impression, having by now cast himself not in the role of an avenging puritan but simply in that of an anxious father trying to save his errant son from corruption.

The trial was fixed for the next Old Bailey Sessions on 3 April, just under a month hence, and it was in this interim that Oscar made the second of his great mistakes. Thinking perhaps that the speed with which the case had been sent for trial indicated that his victory was a foregone conclusion, and thinking also that there was nothing he needed to do before his appearance at the Old Bailey, he allowed himself to be talked by Bosie into a fortnight's holiday at Monte Carlo, using the money they had raised for legal expenses from the Douglas family and the Leversons. That the holiday was not a great success can be judged from Wilde himself, writing two years later to Bosie in *De Profundis*:

At a time when I should have been in London taking wise counsel, and calmly considering the hideous trap in which I had allowed myself to be caught – the boobytrap as your father calls it to the present day – you insisted on my taking you to Monte Carlo, of all revolting places on God's earth, that all day, and all night as well, you might gamble as long as the Casino remained open. As for me – baccarat having no charms for me – I was left alone outside to myself. You refused to discuss even for five minutes the position to which you and your father had brought me. My business was merely to pay your hotel expenses and your losses. The slightest allusion to the ordeal awaiting me was regarded as a bore. A new brand of champagne that was recommended to us had more interest for you.

By the time they got back to London it began to dawn on Wilde that he was in real trouble. Queensberry had used the period of his absence (and his own temporary freedom on bail) to round up a number of the panthers, several of whom were warned by two private detectives acting for the Marquis that unless they cooperated it would be much the worse for them. Ever vulnerable to this kind of pressure, alarmed because the private detectives were known to be ex-policemen, and encouraged by the rather vague promise from Queensberry of a possible reward for telling 'the truth' about Wilde, a number of Alfred Taylor's young renters agreed to give evidence should this be needed. Before the end of March, Queensberry was thus able to adapt his plea to one of justification, announcing that he was not only going to establish that Wilde *had* 'posed as a sodomite' but also that he had actually committed the offence on at least ten different occasions, with dates and names to prove it. So, claimed a jubilant Queensberry now, it was 'in the public interest that the libel on the said Oscar Fingal O'Flahertie Wills Wilde should have been published to the exposure of the true character and habits of the said Wilde, and to the prevention of the further debauching of the liege subjects of our Lady the Queen'.

Alerted as he was to this, Wilde could still have dropped his action and left for the Continent and a decent obscurity – a route chosen by others of the period whose private lives left them no ultimate alternative. Many people encouraged Oscar to take it, among them Frank Harris, whom Oscar had asked to be a witness to the morality of *Dorian Gray*. The two men met, as ever, over lunch at the Café Royal and years later Bernard Shaw, who was also there, recalled the scene for Harris:

That day at the Café Royal, Wilde said he had come to ask you to go into the witness box and testify that *Dorian Gray* was a highly moral work. Your answer was something like this: 'For God's sake, man, put everything on that plane out of your head. You don't realize what is going to happen to you. It is not going to be a matter of clever talk about your books. They are going to bring up a string of witnesses that will put art and literature out of the question. Clarke will throw up his brief. He will carry the case to a certain point; and then, when he sees the avalanche coming, he will back out and leave you in the dock. What you have to do is to cross to France tonight. Leave a letter saying that you cannot face the squalor and horror of a law case; that you are an artist and unfitted for such things. Don't stay here clutching at straws like testimonials to *Dorian Gray*. I tell you I know. I know what is going to happen. I know Clarke's sort. I know what evidence they have got. You must go.' It was no use. Wilde was in a curious double temper. He made no pretence either of innocence or of questioning the folly of his proceedings against Queensberry. But he had an infatuate haughtiness as to the impossibility of his retreating, and as to his right to dictate your course. Douglas sat in silence, a haughty indignant silence, copying Wilde's attitude as all Wilde's admirers did, but quite probably influencing Wilde, as you suggest, by the copy. Oscar finally rose with a mixture of impatience and his grand air, and walked out with the remark that he had now found out who were his real friends; and Douglas followed him, absurdly smaller, and imitating his walk, like a curate following an archbishop.

Wilde's 'infatuate haughtiness' now led him like a lamb to the slaughter: deaf
to all entreaties to flee for his life, or at any rate for his reputation, he remained
insufferably joky. 'I have just been abroad and come home again.' he told another
friend who begged him to return to France. 'One can't keep going abroad unless
one is a missionary, or what comes to the same thing, a commercial traveller.'
This particular brand of gallows humour seldom deserted Oscar in the months to
come. 'Have no fear,' he told an actor called Charles Goodhard, 'the working
classes are with me – to a boy,' while two other actors, Lewis Waller and Allan
Aynesworth (then both appearing in Wilde's West End hits and both understandably worried about the effect the outcome of the trial would have on their respective
runs), meeting Wilde in the street, were more than a little embarrassed when
Oscar asked them if they knew what it was that Queensberry was saying about
him. Shifting uneasily from foot to foot they claimed to have heard nothing.
'Then I'll tell you,' said Oscar. 'He actually had the effrontery to say that *The
Importance of Being Earnest* was better acted than *An Ideal Husband*. Naturally
I had to sue.'

But to Queensberry it was still far from a joke. In some fury, having discovered
that the rest of his family were all siding with Oscar and indeed part-financing his
action, the Marquis wrote: 'You must all be mad, and if you choose to make
enquiries you will find that the whole town has been reeking of this hideous
scandal of Oscar Wilde for the last three years.'

On his return from Monte Carlo, Oscar had gone to live not at Tite Street but at
another of the many hotels which now seemed to be his natural home – this time
the one on Holborn Viaduct. Two days before the first Old Bailey trial he did
however take both Constance and Bosie to a performance of *The Importance of
Being Earnest*, at which the latter two met for the last time. Bosie noticed that
'she was very much agitated and when I said goodnight to her at the door of the
theatre she had tears in her eyes.' It seems fair to assume that she and Oscar had
not been living together as man and wife for some time; nor is there any indication
that she had been consulted about the action he was now taking, action which
would shortly mean the end of their life as a family. It would appear however
from Bosie's account that she already had a good idea of what was coming and
that she was soon to be, in her own words, the 'unhappiest woman in London'.

One last series of events, this one totally beyond the control of Oscar or any of
those supposedly helping him at the time, served to set Queensberry's trial up in a
light thoroughly unfavourable to Oscar himself. Lewis Broad explains a complex
but deeply unfortunate chain of accidental circumstances:

Chance, working through a French journalist employed in London, gave a new twist
to the scandal of the case that had a bearing on Wilde's ultimate fate. By a confusion
of names, the journalist was summoned to serve on the Grand Jury which, under the
old procedure, had to give preliminary consideration to an indictment and return a

true bill before an accused person could be put on trial at the assizes. The journalist did not decline the opportunity to take part in so celebrated a case, and thus he came to hear the name mentioned of Lord Rosebery, who had not long succeeded the aged Gladstone as Prime Minister. In his ranting letters Queensberry had accused Rosebery of having a bad influence on his oldest son. He was writing in a political sense, but the Frenchman, mistaking the meaning, thought that Rosebery's morals were at fault. Proceedings before a Grand Jury could not be reported in the English press, but there was no bar abroad. So, the journalist telegraphed a report to his newspaper that the Prime Minister of England was implicated in the Wilde scandal, a report that was quickly spread in the continental press; by this means it became the talk of London clubs, to the vast annoyance of Ministers of the Crown.

The Queensberry trial opened in a blaze of publicity. With Sir Edward Clarke for the prosecution were Charles Mathews and the young Travers Humphreys, while appearing for the defence with Edward Carson were Charles and Arthur Gill. Yet another QC was holding a 'watching brief' for the two Douglas brothers, and the public gallery seemed full of Oscar's supporters, all fashionable London come to hear some of the celebrated repartee for which at the Haymarket they had had to pay good money.

Oscar arrived in a carriage and pair, and walked into court chatting confidently to Clarke. Queensberry presented by contrast a lonely figure in the dock, though he was soon invited by the judge to take a chair just in front of it. There was now little trace in Queensberry's manner of the 'mad Marquis' who had stormed into Tite Street and prowled 'like an ape' around the St James's a few weeks earlier; instead he was at pains to keep a low profile as the 'wronged father' anxiously trying to save his son's reputation. Already perhaps aware of this, Clarke and Wilde had decided that Alfred Douglas should not be called as a witness, despite the fact that he was only too willing to give evidence against his hated father. It would look bad, thought Clarke, to have Queensberry attacked by his own child, and quite apart from that the legal argument was not really concerned with what Bosie or even with what Oscar thought of the Marquis; it was concerned purely and simply with whether or not the Marquis's libel could be justified in law.

At this first trial Oscar was of course the accuser, not the accused, and he seems to have relished his role, seeing it as the opportunity for an extended personal appearance in front of an enthusiastic audience, the chance to expand his philosophy of art forgiving all else, and the occasion for his beloved Bosie's long-awaited revenge on the father who was 'such a funny little man'.

But not everyone saw it quite like that. Queensberry genuinely felt now that it was his duty to bring Wilde to justice, however much personal dislike and even perhaps a curious kind of jealousy over Bosie's affections were mixed up in that feeling. The establishment, in the shape of an ex-Tory Lord Chancellor (Halsbury) simply wanted the whole mess cleared up as legally and swiftly as possible – though by now His Lordship and a good many others had an increasingly clear idea that the mess concerned Oscar rather than Queensberry. For London at large, it was just the latest in a long line of high-society legal scandals of the late nineteenth century (Parnell, Dilke, Tranby Croft, Campbell), and one which few expected to end with accuser and accused virtually changing places in court.

It opened ordinarily enough: Clarke for the prosecution made a lengthy speech in praise of Wilde's work and reputation, touching briefly upon the friendship between Oscar and Bosie but describing none of its details. He then related the events at the Albemarle Club, calling the hall porter to testify that Queensberry had indeed given him the 'somdomite' card produced in evidence, and eventually he called Oscar to the stand. After a further brief resumé of his life, including the early meetings with Queensberry, Clarke simply asked if there was any truth at all in the Marquis's new charges concerning Oscar's conduct 'with different persons'. Wilde said there was not, Clarke sat down, and Carson rose to cross-examine.

The trouble started at once. Oscar, a congenital liar (like his Mother) about the date of his birth, had told the court that he was born in October 1856, and was therefore now thirty-eight. Carson rapidly proved that he had been born in October 1854 and was therefore now forty. It was a small, insignificant lie, and Oscar soon rose above it – but it was also a careless and stupid lie to have risked, knowing the ease with which birth certificates could even then be obtained, and it created a less than dazzling first impression on the jury.

Carson moved on at length to Oscar's one and only novel:

CARSON: This is your introduction to *Dorian Gray*: 'There is no such thing as a moral or an immoral book. Books are well written or badly written. That is all.' That expresses your view?

WILDE: My view on art, yes.

CARSON: Then I take it that no matter how immoral a book may be, if it is well written it is, in your opinion, a good book?

WILDE: Yes, if it were well written so as to produce a sense of beauty, which is the highest sense of which a human being can be capable. If it were badly written it would produce a sense of disgust.

CARSON: Then a well-written book putting forward perverted moral views may be a good book?

WILDE: No work of art ever puts forward views. Views belong to people who are not artists.

CARSON: A perverted novel might be a good book?

WILDE: I do not know what you mean by a perverted novel.

CARSON: Then I will suggest *Dorian Gray* as open to the interpretation of being such a novel.

WILDE: That could only be to brutes and illiterates. The views of Philistines on art are incalculably stupid.

Oscar was clearly ahead now, and beginning fatally to enjoy himself on the stand. 'You talk in *Dorian Gray* about one man adoring another,' said Carson. 'Did you ever adore a man?' 'No,' replied Oscar, 'I've never adored anyone but myself.' Laughter in court.

This was what Wilde had expected; this was why he had been so adamant when asked by Frank Harris why on earth he was going to risk an appearance before a jury. Oscar even saw himself, in this brief hour of triumph, as the lone defender of the artist's freedom, sent into the box to speak up for all other artists suffering under the narrow-minded restrictions of the Philistines.

Doggedly, Carson continued to have extracts from *Dorian Gray* read to the court, but his discussion of them with Wilde remained almost totally academic, rather as though two Oxbridge dons (one liberal, with a sense of humour, the other more querulous and impossibly strait-laced) were discussing the essays of some gifted but controversial pupil. It was a discussion as safely removed from reality as a review in the *Pall Mall Gazette*, and realizing perhaps that it was leading very slowly nowhere Carson changed his attack, turning the attention of the court away from the novel towards one of Oscar's letters – the one to Bosie about his 'red rose-leaf lips':

WILDE: A beautiful letter. It is a poem. I was not writing an ordinary letter. You might as well cross-examine me as to whether *King Lear* or a sonnet of Shakespeare was proper.

CARSON: Apart from art, Mr Wilde?

WILDE: I cannot answer apart from art.

CARSON: Suppose a man who was not an artist had written this letter, would you say it was a proper letter?

WILDE: A man who was not an artist could not have written that letter.

CARSON: Why?

WILDE: Because nobody but an artist could write it. He certainly could not write the language unless he were a man of letters.

CARSON: I can suggest, for the sake of your reputation, that there is nothing very wonderful in this 'red rose-leaf lips' of yours.

WILDE: A great deal depends upon the way it is read.

CARSON: 'Your slim-gilt soul walks between passion and poetry.' Is that a beautiful phrase?

WILDE: Not as you read it, Mr Carson. You read it very badly.

CARSON: I do not pretend to be an artist. When I hear you give evidence I am glad I am not.

CLARKE (intervening): I don't think my learned friend should talk like that. (To Wilde) Pray do not criticize my friend's reading again.

This, then, was the mood of that first day in court, and when it ended Oscar was in little doubt that he would emerge victorious. Indeed that night, from his Holborn Viaduct hotel, he cabled Ada Leverson: 'Everything is very satisfactory.'

The next day, 4 April, the mood changed. Carson abandoned all attempts to pin Oscar down on his writing; he also abandoned his attempts to impugn the lack of morality expressed by Oscar through his characters. He had spent one whole day treading warily around Wilde, ignoring or deliberately misunderstanding references in the letters to 'renters', and allowing Oscar to score obvious laughs with lines about an Oxford magazine (*The Chameleon*) to which he had contributed at Bosie's request being 'worse than immoral – it was badly written'. Now, however, Carson started to go in for the kill, turning his and the court's attention away from Wilde's writing and towards his other loves.

Having established at the end of the first day that Wilde still denied each and every one of the liaisons listed in mitigation of the libel by Queensberry, Carson started the following morning to list some names. Alfred Taylor, for one. And Charles Parker. And Alfred Wood. And William Parker. And a valet called Scarfe. And Edward Shelley. And Charles Mason. And Alphonse Conway. And how about a newspaper boy? ('That,' said Oscar wittily, 'is the first I've heard of his connection with literature.') By now, two things were clear to the court: first that these were not simply names drawn at random out of a hat, but listed for some purpose, and second that they all came from a social class definitely inferior to Oscar's own. These were the kind of men that no literary gentleman would ever know by name; yet Oscar did. How?

Carson pressed his advantage, raising the issue of Wood's attempt at blackmail and describing Taylor's 'house with heavy curtains' in Little College Street. Why, Carson asked repeatedly, did Oscar choose to consort with men like Charlie Parker? What could they possibly have had in common?

In one of his best answers (there were many, even on the second day) Oscar explained: 'I like people who are young, bright, happy, careless and original. I do not like them sensible, and I do not like them old; I don't like social distinctions of any kind, and the mere fact of youth is so wonderful to me that I would sooner talk to a young man for half an hour than be cross-examined by an elderly QC.'

But Carson was still not to be deterred; like a dog worrying a bone he went on at Wilde, asking about his rooms in St James's Place, about the cigarette case he'd once given Charlie Parker, and about Taylor's arrest in the previous summer. Then, towards mid-afternoon, Carson began to ask about Walter Grainger, a sixteen-year-old Oxford youth who had once served Bosie as a valet there and who, at Bosie's insistence, Wilde had taken into the cottage at Goring during their first summer together.

CARSON: Did you ever kiss Grainger?
WILDE: Oh dear no. He was a peculiarly plain boy. He was unfortunately extremely ugly. I pitied him for it.
CARSON: Was that the reason you did not kiss him?
WILDE: Oh, Mr Carson! You are pertinently insolent.

CARSON: Did you say that in support of your statement that you never kissed him?
WILDE: No. It is a childish question.
CARSON: Did you ever put that forward as a reason why you never kissed the boy?
WILDE: Not at all.
CARSON: Why, sir, did you mention that this boy is extremely ugly?
WILDE: For this reason! If I were asked why I did not kiss a door-mat I should say because I do not like to kiss door-mats. I do not know why I mentioned that he was ugly except that I was stung by the insolent question you put to me and the way you have insulted me throughout this hearing ...

At this point the transcripts indicate Wilde becoming increasingly incoherent; Carson's prodding had at last drawn blood. He rounded off his cross-examination with a few comparatively innocuous questions, and then sat down, leaving Clarke to try and pick up the pieces in his re-examination. Clarke failed however to retrieve more than a few of Oscar's lesser slips, and soon Carson was back on his feet making his opening speech for the defence.

It would be his intention, he said, to show that the Marquis of Queensberry had simply been doing everything in his power to extract his errant son from the clutches of a man who had openly befriended such unsavoury types as Charlie Parker, and who had actually visited Taylor's 'shameful den' in Westminster. Then, as the court was about to rise at the end of the second day, Carson played his ace: it would also, he announced, be his intention to call the man Wood (Wilde's would-be blackmailer, to whom he had given the money for a passage to America), since he was now back in the country and prepared to give evidence about the precise nature of his meeting with Oscar.

Wilde was now forced to accept the unacceptable. Even though he had actually seen in advance of the trial the names of those Queensberry said he would be calling to support his plea of justification, he somehow had never really believed that any of them would turn up in court. Now he did. Returning to his Holborn Viaduct hotel he sent a nervous message to Constance in Chelsea ('Allow no one to enter my bedroom or sitting room – except servants ... see no one but your friends'), and then awaited the third day's proceedings.

They began with Carson again on his feet, continuing his relentless listing of the men who would be called to testify. Oscar waited outside the courtroom itself (causing a number of eyebrows to shoot up in the public gallery), and after Clarke had heard the rest of Carson's opening address he left to confer with his client. There was now, said Clarke in some distress, no hope at all of a Guilty verdict. If, moreover, the presence of Taylor, Wood and the others on the witness stand was to be avoided, Wilde's charge would have to be withdrawn at once. There was then a chance that the matter would be allowed to drop, whereas if the men were called Clarke now saw the arrest of Oscar as almost inevitable.

Wilde agreed immediately. Clarke returned to the courtroom, having told

Oscar that there was no need for him to stay in the building any longer – the nearest Clarke could approach a direct hint that the sooner Oscar got out not only of there but also of the country the better it would be for his own future. Taking his time, Clarke then asked the judge for permission to address the court:

I think it must have been present in your Lordship's mind that those who represent Mr Wilde have before them a very terrible anxiety. They cannot conceal from themselves that the judgement that might be formed on the literature and upon the conduct that had been admitted might not improbably induce the jury to say that Lord Queensberry in using the word 'posing' was using a word for which there was sufficient justification ... a verdict given by the jury at the end of all the evidence might be regarded as conclusive on all parts of the case. Therefore [to avoid] investigation of matters of a most appalling character we are willing to submit to a verdict having reference to the literary part of the case.

The judge was not having that. The verdict, he said, must be Guilty or Not Guilty, with no terms or limitations imposed by the prosecution.

CARSON: The verdict (of Not Guilty) will then be that the plea of justification is proved and the words on Lord Queensberry's card were published to the public benefit.
CLARKE: The verdict will be Not Guilty.
JUDGE: The verdict will be Not Guilty, but it is arrived at by that process.

Queensberry thus achieved a total acquittal which at the same time presupposed the guilt or at least the indictability of Oscar on charges that were by no means of a purely literary nature and now even concerned 'the public benefit', whatever that might have been. There was applause in court as the verdict was announced by the foreman of the jury.

Oscar himself drove back to the Holborn Viaduct hotel, where he was immediately joined by Bosie, his brother and the faithful Robbie Ross. From there Oscar dispatched a letter to the *Evening News*, one last pathetic attempt to save his face:

It would have been impossible for me to have proved my case without putting Lord Alfred Douglas in the witness-box against his father. Lord Alfred Douglas was extremely anxious to go into the box, but I would not let him do so. Rather than put him in so painful a position I determined to retire from the case, and to bear on my own shoulders whatever ignominy and shame might result from my prosecuting Lord Queensberry.

But nobody really managed to believe that this alone was the cause of Oscar's retreat, least of all Wilde himself, as he sat apparently immobilized in the hotel. The one thing for it now was to get to Victoria and the boat-train to Calais, and yet that was now the one thing Oscar could not bring himself to do. All his friends urged it: George Wyndham, Bosie's cousin, even sent word from the House of Commons, and messages came from others, but all in vain. The trauma of the last two days had left Wilde in a state of shock and suspended animation, unable to make up his mind to do anything at all beyond sending Ross to tell Constance the news.

Russell, Queensberry's solicitor, acted more quickly. Although he had made it clear in court that his client would not be taking the initiative in any criminal prosecution of Wilde, the moment the jury's verdict was in he sent all his papers from the trial, together with the statements of the witnesses who had not been called, to the Hon. Hamilton Cunffe, Director of Public Prosecutions.

Cunffe, whether just behaving in the stately manner required of his high office or more considerately giving Oscar time to catch the boat train, proceeded quite slowly. He asked first of all to see Russell; then he asked to see the police, who in the meantime had sent a detective to fetch the Chief Metropolitan Magistrate from Bow Street. Meanwhile at the House of Commons the Attorney-General was already discussing the case with the then Home Secretary, later Prime Minister, Herbert Asquith, but they too took their time.

By now it was late afternoon, and Oscar could comfortably have been on the boat-train. In fact, he had got no further away than the Cadogan Hotel, where Bosie had taken rooms a week or two earlier. There he sat, drinking hock and seltzer, and simply waiting for what he must have known was going to happen.

The Chief Metropolitan Magistrate returned to Bow Street about five o'clock, and there signed a warrant of arrest. A reporter from the *Evening News* who had waited at Bow Street then hastened round to the Cadogan to tell Oscar, who 'went grey in the face' but still showed no desire to stir. By now Reggie Turner was with him, so was Bosie, and Robbie Ross was back from breaking the news to Constance. They waited another hour and a half, then came a knock on the door and the arrest of Oscar Wilde at the Cadogan Hotel, an event later and immortally described in a poem by John Betjeman:

> He sipped at a weak hock and seltzer
> As he gazed at the London skies
> Through the Nottingham lace of the curtains
> Or was it his bees-winged eyes?
>
> To the right and before him Pont Street
> Did tower in her new built red,
> As hard as the morning gaslight
> That shone on his unmade bed,
>
> 'I want some more hock in my seltzer,
> And Robbie, please give me your hand –
> Is this the end or the beginning?
> How can I understand?

'So you've brought me the latest *Yellow Book*
And Buchan has got in it now;
Approval of what is approved of
Is as false as a well-kept vow.

'More hock, Robbie – where is the seltzer?
Dear boy, pull again at the bell!
They are all little better than cretins
Though this *is* the Cadogan Hotel

'One astrakhan coat is at Willis's –
Another one's at the Savoy,
Do fetch my morocco portmanteau,
And bring them on later, dear boy.'

A thump, and a murmur of voices –
('Oh why must they make such a din?')
As the door of the bedroom swung open
And TWO PLAIN CLOTHES POLICEMEN came in:

'Mr Woilde, we 'ave come for tew take yew
Where felons and criminals dwell:
We must ask yew tew leave with us quoietly
For this *is* the Cadogan Hotel.'

He rose, and he put down *The Yellow Book*.
He staggered – and, terrible-eyed,
He brushed past the palms on the staircase
And was helped to a hansom outside.

It did not happen precisely like that, of course. Oscar was reading not *The Yellow Book* but *Aphrodite,* by his old Parisian friend Pierre Louÿs, wrapped in a yellow dust-jacket, and the two policemen did allow him enough time to write a note to Bosie, who had been sent a few minutes earlier down to the House of Commons to find out from Wyndham what was going on. Oscar's note, which Bosie found when he got back to an empty Cadogan bedroom, read: 'I will be at Bow Street Police Station tonight – no bail possible I am told. Will you ask Percy [Bosie's brother] and George Alexander, and Waller, at the Haymarket, to attend to give bail. Would you also wire Humphreys to appear at Bow Street for me . . . also, come to see me, Ever Yours, Oscar.'

Bosie did as he was asked. Robbie Ross, meanwhile, had sped back to Tite Street to collect a change of clothes to take to Oscar. Arriving there he found Mrs Wilde and the boys already gone away to stay with her family, and Oscar's bedroom and study locked as he had ordered. Breaking in, he grabbed the clothes and some more than usually incriminating letters. Then, having done the best he could (the police would not allow him to deliver the clothes to Oscar at Bow Street), Robbie in a state of near collapse went to his mother, who next day put him on the first boat to Calais ... a boat also taken by Lord Ronald Gower and one or two other men who had reason to think that they would be better off abroad for the duration of the Wilde case, or at any rate until police pressure was taken off establishments like Alfred Taylor's.

Bosie meanwhile was not having much luck with his attempts to raise money for bail from either George Alexander or Lewis Waller, both of whom were still appearing in Wilde's hit comedies but regretted that they did not have such money readily available. That, for the time being, was however the limit of their hostility; stories about backstage Haymarket celebrations at the news of Oscar's arrest have been more than a little exaggerated over the years and seem, like those of 'fallen women' dancing in the streets at the end of the third trial, to have come from the more feverish of the early biographies. Actors are insecure folk at the best of times, and although sporting men like Alexander and Aynesworth would have had little time for Oscar's sexual vagaries they were hardly likely to celebrate an event which would almost certainly have to mean the closure of their shows.

One last event of that day needs to be recalled; at Bow Street, when he was searched by police, Oscar was found to have £200 on him in £5 notes – notes presumably taken out of a bank in one of his more lucid moments when flight seemed a real possiblity and the hock had not taken over. That it was a real possibility, one only forfeited by Oscar's own inertia and a new and maudlin belief that he was doomed if not actually damned, is one of the greater tragedies of the Wilde story.

The following morning, 6 April, Wilde was charged at Bow Street with offences under what became known as the 'blackmailer's charter' namely Section 11 of the Criminal Law Amendment Act, 1885, 'for the protection of minors' – it having been established in court that some of the 'panthers' were less than eighteen. His arrest (while in no fit state to do anything but follow in his befuddled way the two police officers who had gone to collect him from the Cadogan) came as a fair surprise to a number of people connected with the Queensberry case, some of whom clearly thought he would have got safely away to France. Even the Marquis himself wrote to Wilde immediately after his own release in those terms: 'If the country allows you to leave, all the better for the country; but if you take my son with you, I will follow you, wherever you go, and shoot you.'

The country had in effect allowed Oscar to leave and he had not done so. Now it was to visit upon him all the wrath of the English in one of the 'periodical fits of morality' which Macaulay had found so ridiculous in Byron's time seventy years earlier. True, some did behave very well towards Oscar now that the axe had fallen; many others behaved a great deal worse, and a few just watched the fracas with the kind of horrified fascination best expressed by Henry James in his letter of 8 April to Edmond Gosse, himself no great lover of Wilde:

It has been, it is, hideously atrociously dramatic and really interesting – so far as one can say of a thing of which the interest is qualified by such sickening horribility. It is the squalid gratuitousness of it all – the mere exposure – that blurs the spectacle. But the *fall* from nearly twenty years of a really unique kind of 'brilliant' conspicuity (wit, 'art', conversation – one of our two or three dramatists etc) to that sordid prison cell and this gulf of obscenity over which the ghoulish public hangs and gloats – it is beyond the utterance of irony or any pang of compassion! He was never in the smallest degree interesting to me – but this hideous human history has made him so – in a manner.

Editors ran the story for all it was worth, publishing lascivious cartoons of Oscar in a cell alongside stories of stunning irresponsibility, presupposing his guilt on all counts and 'recreating' scenes at Alfred Taylor's Westminster house. ('Was it in a bad neighbourhood?' Wilde was asked, only to reply: 'I know nothing about that – it was near the House of Commons.') That the case remained officially *sub judice* seems to have hindered no single paper in condemning Oscar over the following weekend in what even Frank Harris was moved to describe as 'an orgy of Philistine rancour'. *The Echo* considered Oscar quite simply 'damned and done for', and that was among the most sober reflections of Fleet Street. It would have been hard, by the following Monday morning, to have found in all England, let alone London, twelve good men and true who could honestly say that their thinking about Oscar had not been affected in any way by what they had already read or seen on placards and pamphlets and in page after page of newsprint, let alone what they had heard in idle gossip. This was, for most people outside a small London-and-Oxford coterie of theatre-goers, readers and lecture enthusiasts, their first real introduction to Wilde, and when three weeks later the first of the trials at which he was to be the defendant actually began, the jury which entered the box did so with minds already rather less than totally open.

The case was no longer being directed as a private Queensberry–Wilde affair but instead on behalf of 'the Crown', and its agents went swiftly to work, rounding up Alfred Taylor and giving him a bleak choice: either appear as a witness and give evidence against Wilde, or be charged with Wilde with conspiracy to corrupt the young. To his everlasting credit, Taylor chose the second option, and on the following Thursday both men were bound over for trial by Sir John Bridge, to whom Travers Humphreys applied on Oscar's behalf for bail. His plea was that Wilde had made no attempt to leave London in the few hours after he had been told that a warrant was out for his arrest, but Bridge refused to grant bail to either defendant ('I think there is no worse crime than that with which the prisoners are charged'), and Oscar was sent back to Holloway, where he had been held since the morning after his arrest.

His counsel, Sir Edward Clarke, had written immediately to Charles Humphreys offering to defend Wilde at his trial for nothing, a noble offer considering that Clarke must now have known at least something of the truth of Oscar's position. The ever-faithful Leversons and Mrs Beere also wrote offering to help in any way they could, and Edward Carson distinguished himself by declining to have anything to do with the prosecution of his old Trinity contemporary now that the Wilde case had entered an altogether different dimension from the one for which he had been retained by Queensberry.

But, with Robbie Ross already out of the country, Oscar's one constant friend at this time was Bosie, who paid daily visits to Holloway in what can be considered the finest hour of his friendship, indeed perhaps the only hour of it in which his behaviour was totally above reproach. The visits were not easy, as he himself later recalled:

I saw him every day in the ghastly way that 'visits' are arranged in prisons. The visitor goes into a box, rather like a box in a pawnshop. There is a whole row of these boxes, each occupied by a visitor and opposite, facing each visitor, is the prisoner he is visiting. The two sides of visitors and prisoners are separated by a corridor about a yard in width and a warder passes up and down the corridor. The 'visit' lasts about a quarter of an hour. The visitor and the prisoner have to shout to make their voices heard above the voices of other prisoners and visitors. Poor Oscar was rather deaf. He could hardly hear what I said in the babel. He looked at me with tears running down his cheeks and I looked at him. Such it was, as he told me in every letter he wrote (he wrote every day with clockwork regularity), this interview was the only bright spot in his day. He looked forward to it with pathetic eagerness. The world outside the prison, as represented by the newspapers, was howling for his blood like a pack of wolves.

Bosie's reward was a letter from Oscar to Ada Leverson: 'A slim thing, gold-haired like an angel, stands always at my side. His presence overshadows me. He moves in the gloom like a white flower.' But the comfort of Bosie's presence had to make up for a great deal of misery elsewhere. By now it was becoming all too clear that the wolves were out: Wilde's publisher, John Lane, nervously aware that one of the young men cited in the case (Edward Shelley) had been his office boy, hastily wrote to *The Times* dissociating himself from the case and, as if to make amends, promptly withdrew all Oscar's books from sale.

At the same time, Lewis Waller (at the Haymarket in *An Ideal Husband*) and George Alexander (at the St James's in *The Importance of Being Earnest*) had Wilde's name blacked out of the programmes and posters advertising his plays. Apologists for Alexander later tried to claim that he had only done this in order to keep *The Importance* ... running, in the distinctly curious belief that people

would only come to see it if they did not already know who it was by; this however
still does not explain why when Wilde was later declared bankrupt Alexander
seized the opportunity to buy all rights in *Lady Windermere's Fan* and *The
Importance* ... for a derisory sum, and his name must now be added to the sizeable
list of those whose behaviour in the immediate aftermath of Wilde's arrest left a
great deal to be desired. There was, though, a wonderful irony about the title of
the play with which he replaced *The Importance* ... at the St James's – Henry
Arthur Jones's *Triumph of the Philistines*.

Yet Oscar, as so often, had the last laugh. His other current West End success,
An Ideal Husband, was already due to close at the Haymarket (to make way for
Tree's return from America) at the time of his arrest, and Charles Wyndham had
agreed to let Waller transfer it to his Criterion Theatre. When however he noticed
that Waller too had begun to black Wilde's name off the posters, Wyndham
decreed that unless the author's name was restored to its rightful place on all
programmes and posters he would not take the play in. Wyndham was not, he
added, going to allow any theatre of his to be used to offend a man about to go on
trial, and for the length of Oscar's stay in Holloway '*An Ideal Husband* by Oscar
Wilde' was proclaimed in block letters on all the Criterion's advertising.

Constance meanwhile had gone into hiding, accompanied by Cyril and Vyvyan,
for whom the sensational publicity had meant an abrupt end to their school term.
By now their mother was coming to rely more and more on the predictions of the
'sibyl', Mrs Robinson, to whom as early as 19 April (a week before the trial even
started) Constance was writing in no uncertain terms about her future plans:
'As soon as this trial is over I have to get my judicial separation, or if possible my
divorce in order to get the guardianship of the boys. What a tragedy for him who
is so gifted.'

But now Oscar's greatest and most immediate problem was money. With his
books withdrawn and both his plays soon to close (*An Ideal Husband* lasted less
than a month at the Criterion), the income which had been at its height a few
weeks ago now dwindled rapidly to nothing. Having been refused bail on two
separate occasions, Oscar was now also powerless in Holloway to sort out either
his own defence or his financial affairs. Creditors whom he had failed to pay off
in previous months began to press (motivated partly by an understandable feeling
that if they were to get their money back at all it had to be now, and partly by a
less understandable desire to join in the general hunt for Oscar's blood), and on
24 April a farcical 'sale' was held at Tite Street by Court order.

Then and there a great many of Oscar's manuscripts and other possessions were
simply stolen by the curious who had wandered in off the streets, while a few other
belongings went under the hammer to genuine purchasers, but for a fraction of their
real value. A Whistler drawing went for £6; a poem in Keats's handwriting for
thirty-eight shillings. One or two friends attended the fiasco, including Will

Rothenstein, who bought another painting for £8 and later resold it for many times the price, handing the profit straight back to Wilde.

Other men also did him good turns: over in Paris Robert Sherard, though now being named in much of the publicity surrounding Wilde, and suffering accordingly, went at Oscar's request to see Sarah Bernhardt to ask her to buy *Salomé*. Sarah, according to Sherard, received him graciously, wept at his news of Oscar, regretted she could not afford to buy the rights in *Salomé* but agreed to lend Oscar £400 if Sherard would call back for the money in a day or two. He called back on several occasions, only to be told that Madame Bernhardt was out and had left no message. Sherard was appalled, noting later that she had done herself out of a good deal, since *Salomé* was later to become a valuable dramatic property, but Oscar seemed totally unsurprised at his news: 'Sarah of course did not keep her appointment . . . she never does.' And he remained commendably unperturbed by the behaviour of John Lane and George Alexander in England, whom he described respectively as 'ridiculous' and 'childish', but for whom he reserved none of the hatred he was later to lavish on most members of the Queensberry family, including Bosie.

Meanwhile, in Holloway, Oscar continued to see his solicitors in an attempt to sort out his evidence, though he himself now seemed to regard this as almost a formality. 'What is loathsome to me,' he wrote later, 'is the memory of interminable visits paid by me to the solicitor Humphreys when in the ghastly glare of a bleak room I would sit with a serious face telling serious lies to a bald man till I really groaned and yawned with ennui.'

Two days before the trial was due to begin, Wilde and Clarke decided that it could do their case no possible good to have Bosie in court or even in the country. Accordingly he was sent, reluctantly, to the Terminus Hotel in Calais, though not before he had signed a series of long and defiant letters to the *Star* noting that his friend was about to be handed over not to an impartial jury but to 'the fury of a cowardly and brutal mob'. But from the time of his departure for Calais, Bosie and Oscar were not to meet again for two years and four months, and in that period their friendship – now at the peak of its curiously mercurial intensity – was to suffer some abrupt reversals.

The first of the two trials in which Wilde appeared as a defendant opened at the Old Bailey before Justice Charles on 26 April 1895, and lasted five days. As it began, Clarke tried to get the 'conspiracy' charge dropped, and although this failed initially, Sir Edward did manage during the hearing to get this and several other charges dismissed for the trumped-up frauds they were. He also got one witness dismissed for perjury and another to deny any misconduct on Wilde's part, but these were minor victories concerned with inessentials which the prosecution was using to window-dress an undeniably strong case.

Cross-examined in the box by C. F. Gill for the Crown, Wilde was asked about a poem written by Lord Alfred, a poem about the 'Love that dare not speak its name'. What, asked Gill, was that love? Oscar replied at length:

The Love that dare not speak its name in this century is such a great affection of an elder for a younger man as there was between David and Jonathan, such as Plato made the very basis of his philosophy, and such as you find in the sonnets of Michelangelo and Shakespeare. It is that deep, spiritual affection that is as pure as it is perfect. It dictates and pervades great works of art like those of Shakespeare and Michelangelo, and those two letters of mine, such as they are. It is in this century misunderstood, so much misunderstood, that it may be described as the 'Love that dare not speak its name' and on account of it I am placed where I am now. It is beautiful, it is fine, it is the noblest form of affection. There is nothing unnatural about it. It is intellectual, and it repeatedly exists between an elder and a younger man, when the elder man has intellect, and the younger man has all the joy, hope and glamour of life before him. That it should be so the world does not understand. The world mocks at it, and sometimes puts one in the pillory for it.

It was the best of all Oscar's court-room speeches, and though it had little in fact to do with the case in hand, and still less to do with cigarette cases and panthers and rooms in Westminster, it won for Oscar a brief round of applause and the enthusiasm of Max Beerbohm who, along with such other celebrities as Jerome K. Jerome, was there to hear it. 'Oscar has been quite superb,' Max wrote to Reggie Turner that night:

... his speech about the Love that dares not tell its name was simply wonderful and carried the whole court right away – quite a tremendous burst of applause. Here was this man – who had been for a month in prison and loaded with insults and crushed and buffeted, perfectly self-possessed, dominating the Old Bailey with his fine presence and musical voice. He has never had so great a triumph, I am sure, as when the gallery burst into applause ...

On the night of 29 April, from Holloway, after four long days in the dock, Oscar wrote to Bosie in France:

My dearest boy, This is to assure you of my immortal, my eternal love for you. Tomorrow all will be over. If prison and dishonour be my destiny, think that my love for you and this idea, this still more divine belief, that you love me in return will sustain me in my unhappiness and will make me capable, I hope, of bearing my grief most patiently. Since the hope, nay rather the certainty, of meeting you again in some world is the goal and the encouragement of my present life, ah!, I must continue to live in this world because of that ... I am so happy that you have gone away! I know what that must have cost you. It would have been agony for me to think that you were in England when your name was mentioned in court. I hope you have copies of all my books. All mine have been sold. I stretch out my hands towards you. Oh! may I live to touch your hair and your hands. I think that your love will watch over my life. If I should die, I want you to live a gentle peaceful existence somewhere, with flowers, pictures, books, and lots of work. Try to let me hear from you soon. I am writing you this letter in the midst of great suffering; this long day in court had exhausted me. Dearest boy, sweetest of all young men, most loved and most lovable. Oh! wait for me! wait for me! I am now, as ever since the day we met, yours devoutly and with an immortal love.

Inside or outside the witness box Oscar was nothing if not dramatic, but all was not, in fact, to end the next day. Clarke made an eloquent closing speech asking for 'a renowned and accomplished man of letters' (happily he had not seen the one to Bosie) to be freed of any connection with the 'perjurer and blackmailers' trying to ruin his reputation, and the jury was then sent out; but (and this remains some tribute to Clarke's skill as an advocate) they failed to agree on a verdict. They returned to court to be dismissed on 1 May by an angry Justice Charles who, refusing even now to allow Oscar out on bail, announced at once that there would soon be a retrial – making it clear, by his very speed, that the establishment was determined to get a conviction, if not sooner then certainly later.

Four days afterwards Wilde was grudgingly allowed bail, set at an extortionate £5000 and guaranteed partly by Wilde himself, partly by Bosie's elder brother, partly by the Leversons and partly by an unknown clergyman, the Reverend Stewart Headlam, who had never actually met Oscar but who was convinced he was not getting a fair hearing and felt therefore that bail would better enable the unfortunate man to sort out his own defence.

Wilde took rooms first of all at the Midland Hotel, St Pancras, but was rapidly evicted from there by a nervous manager who had heard that 'Queensberry's mob' had threatened to smash up any hotel which gave him shelter. Oscar, hearing the same story at two or three other hotels, eventually went to his mother's house in Oakley Street, where he found his brother Willie as ever less than helpful. It was Willie who once memorably told Bernard Shaw that Oscar 'was not a man of bad character – you could trust him with a woman anywhere', and already Oscar viewed him as a mixed blessing: 'Willie must be stopped. He tells me that he is defending me all over London. My poor dear brother could compromise a steam engine.'

Frank Harris and Robert Sherard both went to visit Oscar at Speranza's, and both urged him to flee the country. Sperenza however insisted, as did Yeats (another visitor), that he was 'an Irish gentleman' and therefore would do no such thing. There was even dramatic talk of suicide, with Sherard somewhat tactlessly telling Oscar precisely how prussic acid could be made (presumably in the certain knowledge that Oscar had actually no intention of ending his own life), but Sherard does offer us a sad portrait of Wilde during these last two weeks of freedom he would ever spend in England: 'He was lying on a small camp-bedstead in a corner between the fireplace and the wall, and in a glass on a mantelpiece was an arum lily, sere and yellow, which drooped lamentably down over his head. His face was flushed and swollen, his voice was broken, he was a man altogether collapsed.'

Bosie wrote from France, also urging escape immediately and assuring Oscar that his family could well afford to lose the bail money, but the furthest that Oscar was prepared to travel was to the Leversons' house in Courtfield Gardens, in search of the tranquillity that had so eluded him in Oakley Street. Ada had offered to put him up in her nursery until the trial was over, and largely to escape the combined ministrations and advice of mother, brother, Sherard and Harris, Oscar retreated there with some relief – though not before Mrs Leverson had assembled all her servants and offered them each a week's pay in lieu of notice if they chose not to work in a house where Mr Wilde was to be a guest. They all stayed.

Harris later wrote of grandiose plans to have a steam yacht waiting on the Thames at Erith 'like a greyhound at the leash', straining to carry Oscar off to France, but these were pure fantasy and Oscar was in any case now happily installed with the Leversons, as Ada later recalled:

While all our friends as well as the whole of the public were discussing Oscar, no one had any idea that he was under our roof. He made certain rules to avoid any embarrassment to us. He never left the nursery floor till six o'clock. He had luncheon and tea up there and received all his loyal friends there. He never would discuss his troubles before me; such exaggerated delicacy seems today almost incredible. But every day at six he would come down dressed for dinner and would talk to me for a couple of hours in the drawing-room. As always he was most carefully dressed, there was a flower in his buttonhole and he had received his usual daily visit from his old hairdresser, who shaved him and waved his hair as he had been accustomed to do in the past.

Even Constance agreed to visit Oscar at the Leversons, and she too urged an escape, but by now Oscar had sunk back into the lethargy which first overcame him at the Cadogan, and he seemed almost peacefully to be awaiting the third of the Old Bailey trials – either out of a still stubborn belief that he would at the end of it all be acquitted, or simply and more plausibly because he was now past caring. Toulouse-Lautrec also visited Wilde on the eve of the last trial, and his portrait, too, suggests a man of remarkable composure.

On 20 May the third Wilde trial opened at the Central Criminal Court. The Solicitor-General, Sir Frank Lockwood, was now leading for the prosecution, apparently unperturbed by the fact that his wife's nephew, Maurice Schwabe, was one of the young men whom witnesses said they had seen in bed with Oscar. Clarke, still appearing unpaid for Oscar, applied to have his client and Taylor now tried separately, since they were no longer linked by the conspiracy charge. The judge agreed, but insisted on the prosecution's right to try Taylor first – thereby ensuring that the mood of the court would be still less open to doubt when it came to Oscar's turn. Taylor was found guilty on two charges at the end of the second day, and that night an exuberant Queensberry telegraphed to his daughter-in-law: 'Must congratulate on verdict. Cannot on Percy's appearance. Looked like a dug-up corpse. Fear too much madness of kissing. Taylor guilty. Wilde's turn tomorrow, Queensberry.'

The telegram did not, predictably, delight Percy himself, who actually struck his father in St James's Street the next time they met. A full fist-fight developed, and father and son were later charged with disorderly conduct.

Meanwhile Wilde was back in the dock for the last time, and on rather more serious charges than those which now occupied the Queensberry family. The night before his last trial he had written to Bosie explaining his reasons for being there:

I decided that it was nobler and more beautiful to stay. We could not have been together. I did not want to be called a coward or a deserter. A false name, a disguise, a hunted life, all that is not for me, to whom you have been revealed on that high hill where beautiful things are transfigured. O sweetest of all boys, most loved of all loves, my soul clings to your soul, my life is your life, and in all the worlds of pain and pleasure you are my ideal of admiration and joy.

Mr Justice Wills was now the judge, and all the old arguments about Oscar's and the Marquis of Queensberry's behaviour, the house in Little College Street and the acknowledged criminality of many of the witnesses were rehearsed yet again. This time, though, the foreman of the jury did intervene to suggest that as Lord Alfred's name had frequently been mentioned it might perhaps make sense to have him charged with some of the offences. The judge was visibly shocked at the mere suggestion, pointing out sharply that: 'Nothing that can be said either for or against Lord Alfred Douglas must be allowed to prejudice the prisoner; it is a thing we cannot discuss.'

This last trial was also remarkable for other moments: for the way in which Clarke reprimanded the new prosecutor Lockwood (his successor as Solicitor-General) for his determination to get a verdict of 'Guilty' at any price; for the singularly nasty 'stained sheet' evidence offered by Savoy Hotel chambermaids; and also for the final row during the judge's summing-up when, after the foreman's intervention about Douglas, Clarke remarked that the trial 'seemed to be operating as an act of indemnity for all the blackmailers in London'. The jury then retired to consider their verdict for two and a half hours – too long, thought Lockwood, for 'Guilty', and he told Clarke he would be 'dining his man in Paris' the following day.

But that was not to be. When the jury filed back into court shortly before six on the evening of 25 May it was to return a verdict of Guilty on no less than seven of the eight counts. The judge then sent for both defendants:

Oscar Wilde and Alfred Taylor, the crime of which you have been convicted is so bad that one has to put stern restraint upon oneself from describing in language I would rather not use the sentiments that must rise to the breast in every man of honour who has heard the details of the two terrible trials. It is of no use for me to address you.

People who can do these things must be dead to all sense of shame and one cannot hope to produce any effect upon them. It is the worst case I have ever tried. That you, Taylor, kept a kind of male brothel it is impossible to doubt. And that you, Wilde, have been the centre of a circle of extensive corruption of the most hideous kind among young men it is equally impossible to doubt. I shall, under the circumstances, be expected to pass the severest sentence the law allows. In my judgement it is totally inadequate for such a case.

Each man got two years' hard labour. 'And I, my lord?' Oscar called from the dock, 'am I to say nothing?' But Wills waved him away, and Wilde was taken to the cells and then to Pentonville prison to begin his sentence. It was just thirteen weeks since he had found Queensberry's card at the Albemarle and Oscar was still in his forty-first year.

11
READING GAOL...
AND DE PROFUNDIS

—

1895–1897

From Pentonville, Oscar was moved to Wandsworth prison, where he served the first five months of his sentence. During this time, medically certified as fit for light rather than hard labour, and set to sewing mailbags, his suffering was mental rather than physical. Allowed initially to write only one letter in three months, and to speak only for set, short periods each day, he retreated into a kind of desperate gloom which caused at least one newspaper to report that he had finally taken leave of his senses altogether, a view also shared by Constance, who thought he was suffering from 'erotomania' (OED: 'melancholy madness arising from love'), a splendid and typically theatrical disease which Oscar himself would later plead in one of his unsuccessful petitions for early release.

What he was in fact suffering from was nothing more nor less than the full gothic awfulness of an English prison in Victorian times. Those were not the days when homosexuality was viewed with any special interest, understanding or compassion within the prison service, and for Wilde, thrown in solitary confinement into an airless cell with a plank for a bed and nothing to do but sew mailbags and try unsuccessfully to sleep in the few hours for which this was permitted, it was a truly Dickensian punishment unalleviated in any way.

He could not, after all, tell himself that he was in prison for having taken any kind of moral stand apart from that of deciding not to become an exiled fugitive. Nor was he there because of a great and noble romantic passion for Lord Alfred, whom even the judge had refused to consider in evidence; nor for a single defiant action which would later be recognized and win him posthumous glory. He was there, solely and simply, because he had been to bed carelessly with a number of young men few of whom he could now even remember by name. It was, in brief, an ignoble and messy affair, which ill suited the romantic aura with which he had

liked to think his life and career had been invested. Still, for the moment he was
not prepared to lay the blame on Bosie; as he wrote in *De Profundis*:

After my terrible sentence, when the prison-dress was on me, and the prison-house
closed, I sat amidst the ruins of my wonderful life, crushed by anguish, bewildered with
terror, dazed through pain. But I would not hate you. Every day I said to myself 'I
must keep love in my heart today, else how shall I live through the day?' I reminded
myself that you meant no evil, to me at any rate; I set myself to think that you had
but drawn a bow at a venture, and that the arrow had pierced a King between the
joints of the harness. To have weighed you against the smallest of my sorrows, the
meanest of my losses, would have been, I felt, unfair. I determined I would regard you
as one suffering too. I forced myself to believe that at last the scales had fallen from
your long-blinded eyes. I used to fancy, and with pain, what your horror must have
been when you contemplated your terrible handiwork. There were times, even in those
dark days, the darkest of all my life, when I actually longed to console you. So sure was
I that you at last had realized what you had done.

What Bosie had done, of course, was to encourage Oscar to start the proceedings
against Queensberry which Oscar saw now as the root of all his present agony:

Of course once I had put into motion the forces of Society, Society turned on me and
said, 'Have you been living all this time in defiance of my laws, and do you now appeal
to those laws for protection? You shall have those laws exercised to the full. You shall
abide by what you have appealed to.' The result is I am in gaol. And I used to feel
bitterly the irony and ignominy of my position when in the course of my three trials,
beginning at the Police Court, I used to see your father bustling in and out in the hopes
of attracting public attention, as if anyone could fail to note or remember the stable-
man's gait and dress, the bowed legs, the twitching hands, the hanging lower lip, the
bestial and half-witted grin. Even when he was not there, or was out of sight, I used to
feel conscious of his presence, and the blank dreary walls of the great Court-room, the
very air itself, seemed to me at times to be hung with multitudinous masks of that
apelike face. Certainly no man ever fell so ignobly, and by such ignoble instruments,
as I did. I say, in *Dorian Gray* somewhere, that 'a man cannot be too careful in the choice
of his enemies'. I little thought that it was by a pariah that I was to be made a pariah
myself.

But, within a matter of weeks, Wilde began to shift the weight of the blame for
his misfortune off his own shoulders, off even those of Lord Queensberry, and firmly,
on to those of the once 'golden, slim-gilt boy' who was Alfred Douglas. It happened
slowly at first, and for a variety of reasons. First came the problem of Wilde's own
identity:

When first I was put in prison some people advised me to try and forget who I was.
It was ruinous advice. It is only by realizing what I am that I have found comfort of
any kind. Now I am advised by others to try on my release to forget that I have ever
been in a prison at all. I know that would be equally fatal. It would mean that I would

be always haunted by an intolerable sense of disgrace, and that those things that are meant as much for me as for anyone else – the beauty of the sun and the moon, the pageant of the seasons, the music of daybreak and the silence of great nights, the rain falling through the leaves, or the dew creeping over the grass and making it silver – would all be tainted for me, and lose their healing power and their power of communicating joy. To reject one's own experience is to put a lie into the lips of one's own life. It is no less than a denial of the Soul.

But if Wilde was not to reject or to deny his own experiences, then he had to relive them, and the more he relived them in his mind's eye the more clearly Bosie was cast in the role of villain. It was a role others were eager to cast him in, too; his passionate on-off romance with Oscar had after all almost totally blocked both Robbie Ross and Robert Sherard out, denying them access to their old friend. And now, in Oscar's hour of need, it was they who came running.

Bosie chose with his customary insouciance to spend the summer of 1895 on Capri. Robbie however returned from France expressly to be close to Wilde, as did Sherard, who even took rooms close to Wandsworth prison, where he became one of Wilde's very first visitors. The first of all had of course been the prison chaplain, who was less than helpful. 'Did you have morning prayers in your house?' he asked the unhappy Oscar, who replied that they had not. 'Then,' said the chaplain triumphantly, 'you see where you are now' – as if in some wondrous way the absence of morning prayer in Tite Street could somehow explain the vortex of the last three years.

Following the chaplain came a more welcome and helpful visitor, the politician R. B. Haldane, who had known Oscar in happier times, and now took the trouble to see him privately, a privilege he was able to arrange since he then served on the Prison Commission. Haldane discovered that the only book Oscar had been allowed during his first month in Wandsworth was *The Pilgrim's Progress*, which as Oscar said was really not quite enough. He therefore arranged that Oscar should also have Pascal's *Pensées*, Pater's *Renaissance* and several books by Cardinal Newman, though he drew the line at Oscar's request for *Madame Bovary* since Flaubert had dedicated it to the barrister who got him off a charge of obscene publication.

It was in August 1895 that Robert Sherard paid his first visit. 'I noticed that Oscar's hands were disfigured and that his nails were broken and bleeding [the result, presumably, of such prison tasks as crank-turning and oakum-picking] also that his head and face were untidy with growth of hair.' A month later Constance herself went to the prison. By now she had decided to live with her sons on the Continent and to change all their names to Holland in an effort to escape the horrors and the memories which the past few months had held for them too.

But for Oscar, quite apart from the present indignities of life behind bars, the horrors were by no means over. By now he was suffering from chronic diarrhoea, and had perforated an eardrum in a fainting fit one morning in chapel. Nor were things going much better for him outside the walls of Wandsworth: in June, realizing that he was in some danger of not getting his costs paid, Queensberry lodged a bankruptcy petition against Wilde. The receiving order was issued a month later, and in August creditors were told that Wilde's debts amounted to £3500 (of which Queensberry's money, which had caused the order, amounted to only just over £600). But with his plays and books now all withdrawn, and with Wilde's own name having totally disappeared from public view, there was of course no chance that the money could be repaid within the foreseeable future.

In September there was a public examination to which Oscar was brought in handcuffs from Wandsworth, pleased only that Robbie Ross had taken the trouble to be in court and raise his hat as Oscar passed. The court was told that £1500 had already been raised by Wilde's friends, and that the rest would doubtless follow, but the sale of his Tite Street house and of the few belongings which still remained there did not come up to financial expectations, and on 12 November the public examination continued, with Wilde having to list to an impassive Official Receiver the precise nature of his debts and how they had been incurred. By now, Oscar was in no doubt about where to lay the blame for his bankruptcy. He wrote to Bosie in *De Profundis*:

When I tell you that between the autumn of 1892 and the date of my imprisonment I spent with you and on you more than £5000 in actual money, irrespective of the bills I incurred, you will have some idea of the sort of life on which you insisted. Do you think I exaggerate? My ordinary expenses with you for an ordinary day in London – for luncheon, dinner, supper, amusements, hansoms and the rest of it – ranged from £12 to £20, and the week's expenses were naturally in proportion and ranged from £80 to £130. For our three months at Goring my expenses (rent of course included) were £1,340! Step by step with the Bankruptcy Receiver I had to go over every item of my life. It was horrible. 'Plain living and high thinking' was of course not an ideal you could at that time have appreciated, but such extravagance was a disgrace to both of us.

Wilde was further indignant that when his possessions had to be sold, Douglas made no attempt to buy them in for him, nor were their relations inproved by the news, brought to Wilde in prison by Sherard, that Bosie planned to publish some of his letters from Oscar in the *Mercure de France* as part of a heavy-handed attempt to arouse French support for his friend. Even in his present distress Oscar could see that the letters would do nothing but harm to his cause, and that for Bosie to write:

. . . a patronizing and Philistine letter about 'fair play' for a 'man who is down' is all right for an English newspaper. It carries on the old tradition of English journalism in regard to their attitude towards artists. But in France such a tone would have exposed me to ridicule . . . I could not have allowed any article till I had known its aim, temper, mode of approach and the like. In art good intentions are not of the smallest value. All bad art is the result of good intentions.

The passionate love for Bosie which Oscar had expressed in those letters, written on the eve of his imprisonment, had turned within five Wandsworth months to bitter fury, and it could be argued that this seething hatred of Douglas, short-lived though it was to prove, was the one thing which kept Oscar from cracking under the strain of imprisonment. It was to find its eventual outlet in the *De Profundis* letter he wrote to Bosie from Reading gaol in the early months of 1897 (and from which most of the quotations in this chapter are drawn), but for now it was simply allowed to strengthen and take root, encouraged by both Sherard and Ross.

Sherard it was who also acted as go-between for Oscar and Constance, persuading her to visit him in Wandsworth for what she later described as 'the saddest meeting of my life. I could not see him and I could not touch him and I scarcely spoke. Oscar talked of the past, and of his fatal friendship with Lord Alfred Douglas. He told me that if he ever saw him again he would shoot him – so he had better keep away and be satisfied with having marred a fine life. Few people can boast of so much.' There was much talk of shooting that summer. Bosie, on Capri still, heard that Sherard had managed a brief reconciliation between Oscar and Constance and wrote to him in a fury that if anything Sherard said or did should in any way harm his own friendship with Oscar then he would come over and shoot Sherard 'like a dog'.

In a more sober and constructive vein, Haldane continued his visits to Oscar and later remembered how on the first of them:

I put my hand on his prison-dress clad shoulder and said that I used to know him and had come to say something about himself. He had not used fully his great literary gift and the reason was that he had lived a life of pleasure and had not made any subject his own. Now misfortune might prove a blessing to his career for he had got a great subject. I would try to get for him pen and ink and in eighteen months he would be free to produce. He burst into tears and promised to make the attempt.

More helpfully still, Haldane recommended that Wilde should be transferred from Wandsworth to Reading gaol, which was then reckoned generally to be an 'easier' one, largely because it had both a garden and a library where Oscar could be gainfully employed. The move took place in November 1895, and Oscar himself described the awfulness of his train journey from Wandsworth to Reading, one which necessitated a change at Clapham Junction:

From two o'clock till half-past two on that day I had to stand on the centre platform of Clapham Junction, in convict dress and handcuffed, for the world to look at. I had been taken out of the Hospital Ward without a moment's notice being given to me. Of all possible objects I was the most grotesque. When people saw me they laughed. Each train as it came up swelled the audience. Nothing could exceed their amusement. That was of course before they knew who I was. As soon as they had been informed, they laughed still more. For half an hour I stood there in the grey November rain surrounded by a jeering mob. For a year after that was done to me, I wept every day at the same hour and for the same space of time.

This, though, does need to be considered in the light of the high fever of fury and self-pity in which Oscar wrote most of *De Profundis*. Doubtless a train journey anywhere in convict's dress was a terrible experience, especially for a man of Oscar's temperament and reputation; but how could a jeering mob assemble at 2.30 on a wet afternoon at Clapham Junction – and where did all the trains come from in that off-peak period to swell the audience? Doubtless there were a few people around at that time of day, doubtless one or two even recognized Oscar and maybe one lad even said something unkind in his hearing. The event needs to be scaled down, however, before it becomes remotely visible, and the contrast between description and reality, between self-pitying imagination and actuality, gives a microcosmic indication of how best to view the rest of *De Profundis*.

Things did not immediately improve for Oscar in Reading. The then Governor was a Colonel Isaacson, a martinet, and one who took a thoroughly dim view of men of Wilde's sexual persuasions. He therefore punished Oscar for minor or imaginary transgressions of the prison code whenever possible. Oscar meanwhile, tutored by Sherard, was doing his best to overcome his surroundings, helped along in his fury by the curious tactlessness of Bosie, who from Capri did no more than send his regards via a solicitor, and even then used the pseudonym 'Prince Fleur-de-Lys'. 'You were,' wrote Oscar icily in *De Profundis*, 'no doubt right to communicate with me under an assumed name. I myself, at that time, had no name at all.'

Oscar was in fact known as 'C3.3', after the number of his cell, which was the third along on the third landing of C block, and it was under that name that he published the last and by far the best of all his poems, 'The Ballad of Reading Gaol'. The poem was actually written at Berneval, during the summer of 1897, but its inspiration derived from the arrival at Reading gaol a year earlier of Trooper C. T. Wooldridge, charged with (and later executed there for) the murder of his young wife in a fit of jealous rage. Haldane regarded the poem as the redemption of Wilde's promise to use his prison term to explore the 'great literary gift' that Haldane, presumably no great theatregoer, thought Wilde had thus far wasted. However painful the exercise, it does undoubtedly represent Wilde's poetic gift at its brief peak:

> In Reading gaol by Reading town
> There is a pit of shame,
> And in it lies a wretched man
> Eaten by teeth of flame,
> In a burning winding-sheet he lies,
> And his grave has got no name.

And there, till Christ call forth the dead,
In silence let him lie;
No need to waste the foolish tear,
Or heave the windy sigh:
The man had killed the thing he loved
And so he had to die.

And all men kill the thing they love,
By all let this be heard,
Some do it with a bitter look,
Some with a flattering word,
The coward does it with a kiss,
The brave man with a sword!

But there were other things to occupy Wilde's mind at Reading apart from the fate of Trooper Wooldridge – his own peace of mind, for a start. In February 1896 Constance had again travelled from Genoa to see Oscar behind bars, this time to bring him the sad news that his mother had just died of pneumonia. Oscar had not been able to write to Speranza since the trials (his 'allowance' of outgoing letters being largely consumed by business correspondence with Sherard, Ross or his solicitor), and he was bowed down still lower at the news of her death:

I loved and honoured her. Her death was so terrible to me that I, once a lord of language, have no words in which to express my anguish and my shame. Never, even in the most perfect days of my development as an artist, could I have had words fit to bear so august a burden, or to move with sufficient stateliness of music through the purple pageant of my incommunicable woe. She and my father had bequeathed me a name they had made noble and honoured not merely in Literature, Art, Archaeology and Science, but in the public history of my own country in its evolution as a nation. I had disgraced that name eternally. I had made it a low byword among low people. I had dragged it through the very mire. I had given it to brutes that they might make it brutal, and to fools that they might turn it into a synonym for folly. What I suffered then, and still suffer, is not for pen to write or paper to record.

By now Oscar was convinced that he was cracking up, and he sent two petitions to the Home Office which were masterpieces of agonized complaint:

The petitioner is now keenly conscious of the fact that while the three years preceding his arrest were from the intellectual point of view the most brilliant years of his life (four plays from his pen having been produced on the stage with immense success, and played not merely in England, America and Australia, but in almost every European capital, and many books that excited much interest at home and abroad having been published), still that during the entire time he was suffering from the most horrible form of erotomania, which made him forget his wife and children, his high social position in London and Paris, his European distinction as an artist, the honour of his name and family, his very humanity itself, and left him the helpless prey of the most revolting passions, and of a gang of people who for their own profit ministered to them, and then drove him to his hideous ruin. It is under the ceaseless apprehension lest this insanity, that displayed itself in monstrous sexual perversion before, may now extend to the entire nature and intellect, that the petitioner writes this appeal which he earnestly entreats may at once be considered.

Wilde's appeal to the Home Office to let him off the second year of his sentence was accompanied by a curt note from Isaacson to the effect that Oscar had put on weight since his arrival at Reading and showed no discernible traces of insanity. Nevertheless the Home Office, urged on by other pleas from Sherard and Harris (to which both Beerbohm and Shaw gave their support), thought it worth investigating, and sent two prison experts on mental health from Broadmoor to have a look at Oscar. Unluckily, they found him gossiping cheerfully with some other patients in the infirmary, and concluded that he should serve out his second year as sentenced. 'I am dazed with a dull sense of pain,' wrote Oscar when he heard the news, but by now the fearful Isaacson had been replaced as Governor at Reading by 'that good and kind fellow Major Nelson', and Oscar was even able to start work on a few new epigrams.

Constance had now decided against her family's advice, which was to get an immediate divorce, and resolved to settle instead for a deed of separation which would give her custody of Cyril and Vyvyan in return for a promise that she would pay Oscar £150 a year from her own private money so long as he agreed not to go back to live with Lord Alfred Douglas after his release.

For the moment, that seemed highly unlikely: already, in this summer of 1896, Oscar was writing to Robbie Ross asking him to retrieve 'letters, a gold cigarette case, a pearl chain and an enamelled locket' from the now hated Bosie:

The idea that he is wearing or in possession of anything I gave him is peculiarly repugnant to me. I cannot of course get rid of the revolting memories of the two years I was unlucky enough to have him with me, or of the mode by which he thrust me into the abyss of ruin and disgrace to gratify his hatred of his father and other ignoble passions. But I will not have him in possession of my letters or gifts. Even if I get out of this loathsome place I know there is nothing before me but the life of a pariah – of disgrace and penury and contempt – but at least I will have nothing to do with him nor allow him to come near me.

Other friends now began to rally round, including More Adey and Adela Schuster, the latter a lady who had given Oscar £1000 during the trials for no other reason than that his work had given her pleasure. (The money went, rather against Oscar's will, to repay some of his debt to the Leversons.) Sherard was still visiting with news of the outside world, and there were at last some glimmerings of light from there:

in Paris, Lugné-Poë had staged *Salomé* in February with great success (though little financial reward to Oscar, since the Official Receiver was still collecting what he could), and Wilde saw this, correctly, as a sign that in France his reputation was in better shape – a realization which must in part have conditioned his subsequent determination to live out the rest of his life there.

The winter of 1896–7 saw more frequent visits: Ross, Harris, Adey, the Leversons, Sherard and Charles Ricketts all made the short train journey to Reading, and Ross continued to worry about Oscar's appearance, noting streaks of grey in the hair and even the beginning of a bald patch. Oscar now began calling these visits his 'at homes', just as he would later describe his incarceration as 'a spell in the country', and it was evident that at last he was beginning to recapture a sense of humour. Such hatred and bitterness as he reserved for Bosie was to be channelled into *De Profundis*, the fifty-thousand-word complaint Oscar wrote him between January and March 1897 on paper thoughtfully provided by Major Nelson. What emerged from the labour of those months was a masterpiece of vitriolic abuse in which Bosie, and Bosie alone, was blamed for every sordid aspect of the situation in which Oscar now found himself while he, Bosie, floated freely over the Continent in search of new pleasures.

It was, to say the least, a little unfortunate that in the eighteen months since the trials Bosie had neither visited nor written to his old friend, though the intervention of Sherard and Ross had admittedly at no time encouraged him to do so. Nevertheless, by the time of *De Profundis* Wilde was on the up and up again. Sir Edward Clarke had agreed to lend his name to yet another petition for his release, and there had been some discreet gifts from Laurence and A. E. Housman, as well as from Max Beerbohm, who had been appalled to discover, on a visit to the office of the detectives in charge of the Wilde case, his own cartoon of a bloated Oscar hanging on the wall as if in evidence. But although Oscar now knew that he was not totally without honour or love in his own country, *De Profundis* still became both a letter of accusation and a defence for himself. Was it not all Bosie's fault that he was now 'in the lowest mire of Malebolge . . . between Gilles de Retz and the Marquis de Sade' while Queensberry had emerged as the hero of the hour, sure of a place 'among the kind, pure-minded parents of Sunday-school literature'? Was it not all Bosie's fault, the whole tragic waste of Wilde's time, talent and indeed life?

But the saddest aspect of *De Profundis*, quite apart from the bitchy, querulous, waspish image it offers of its author, is that it never reached its target. Wilde wanted the original sent straight to Bosie with a copy to Robbie Ross, but the prison commissioners ruled that it could not leave Reading until Oscar did. He thereupon gave the only copy of it to Ross, who eventually published it after his death in a hopelessly truncated version, having cut all references to Bosie and thus destroyed its purpose altogether. The original manuscript was then lodged by Ross in the British Museum in 1909. A still incomplete version was published by Vyvyan Holland in 1949, and the final and total text only emerged in 1961, just sixty years after Wilde's death and sixteen after that of Lord Alfred Douglas.

Although *De Profundis* did not totally succeed in working off Wilde's pent-up fury in prison, the last six months of his stay there were infinitely the most pleasant. He had now been taken off all but the lightest of library duties, and was being courteously treated by the new governor, who took the trouble to tell Oscar personally that one of his aunts had died and that, by the way, Poynter had become President of the Royal Academy. 'I am grateful to you,' replied Oscar, 'for telling me about my poor aunt, but you really should have broken the news about Poynter more gently.'

But for most of Oscar's last weeks in Reading he was left in the tender care of Warder Martin, whom he introduced to the wonders of literary criticism and who later wrote: 'What the poet was before he went to prison I care not. What he may have been after he left prison I know not. One thing I know, however, that while in prison he lived the life of a saint, or as near that holy state as poor mortal can ever hope to attain.'

Martin was later dismissed from the prison service for giving biscuits to a child, and Wilde wrote a stirring letter in his defence to the *Daily Chronicle*, but there are indications that in these last few months, despite all the protestations of *De Profundis*, and Warder Martin's convictions of sanctity, Oscar had slipped back into his old sexual interests. Martin, asked years later about Wilde's prison friendships, replied briskly: 'I never did night duty,' but in the same letter he mentioned notes delivered from Oscar to young prisoners, to many of whom Wilde also sent a little money on his release.

Other, and angrier, letters were written in this final period of his sentence to Robbie Ross and More Adey ('letters from an idiot to lunatics' Oscar later called the correspondence), since in his view they had bungled the arrangements with Constance's lawyers over the children and a settlement. Nor did Frank Harris endear himself to Oscar by arriving at Reading fresh from some faintly suspect South African mission with the news that he now had £20,000 and would give £500 of it as a present to Oscar. When the cheque came, there was just £450 missing from it.

But all this was forgotten when, on 18 May 1897, Oscar finally got his release. Two reporters at the gates of Reading Gaol watched him leave in a cab for Twyford Station, from where he caught the London train and spent the night at Pentonville, since regulations insisted that he should be released from the same prison to which Judge Wills had originally committed him twenty-four months earlier. At 6.15 next morning Oscar was collected from there in a cab by More Adey and taken to 31 Upper Bedford Place, the Bloomsbury home of Stewart Headlam, the clergyman who had stood bail for him and who was generally reckoned to be so far away from the centre of Wilde's circle that his house would escape any Press attention.

There, on his first morning of freedom, Oscar bathed, changed and breakfasted. Soon afterwards, Ada Leverson came to call. 'My dear Sphinx!' exclaimed Oscar, 'how marvellous of you to know exactly the right hat to wear to welcome a friend who has been away! You can't have got up, you must have sat up.'

12
DEATH OF A POET

—

1897–1900

At the time of his release, Oscar was generally reckoned to be looking better than he had for years. 'His face had lost all its coarseness,' wrote Robbie Ross, 'and he looked as he must have looked at Oxford in the early days before I knew him, and as he only looked again after death.'

Before his departure from Reading, Wilde had smuggled out a letter to another old friend, Reggie Turner, complaining that despite all their promises neither Robbie nor Harris nor the Leversons had really come up with enough money for him to live on in the years to come, though there had been an offer from at least one American journalist of 'any money he liked' in return for an interview. Wilde turned that down in suitably flamboyant language ('Is it not appalling? I who am maimed, ill, altered in appearance so that no one can hardly recognize me, broken-hearted, ruined, disgraced, a leper and a pariah to men – I am to be gibbeted for the pleasure of the public!') and went on to tell Reggie of his plans to settle in 'some seaside place' abroad. A day or two later he added, again in a letter to Reggie, that he would henceforth be calling himself Mr Melmoth, after the hero of a novel by his great-uncle (*Melmoth the Wanderer*) – a pseudonym suggested in fact by Robbie.

But Reggie was not there to greet Oscar on his release ('Were my presence to be made known by any means to my people my allowance would be stopped'), though he did agree to travel to Dieppe with Robbie, there to greet Oscar on his arrival and to present him with a silver dressing-case bearing the initials 'S.M.' for Sebastian Melmoth, Oscar's new name.

Having breakfasted in Bloomsbury with the Sphinx and other London friends, however, Oscar began to have second thoughts about Dieppe. Instead of heading straight for the boat-train, he sent a message by cab to the Jesuits at Farm Street, asking them to take him in for a six-month retreat. They replied with an immediate refusal, offering the rather dubious explanation that such a retreat would have to be thought about and prepared for at least a year in advance. Oscar must have known what this answer would be before he even sent the request; Ada Leverson reports however that he 'burst into tears', recovering later in the day in time to pay a fleeting visit to Hatchards (where he was recognized) to buy some books en route to Croydon and then the train for Newhaven and Dieppe. By now they had missed the afternoon sailing, so Oscar and More Adey, who was accompanying him, spent several hours in a hotel at Newhaven before catching the night boat. These were the last hours Oscar ever spent on British soil.

Early the following morning, as the ferry sailed into Dieppe, Robbie Ross was on the quayside:

Wilde talked till nine o'clock when I insisted on going to lie down. We all met at twelve for déjeuner, all of us exhausted except Wilde. In the afternoon we drove to Arques and sat down on the ramparts of the castle. He enjoyed the trees and the grass and the country scents and sounds in a way I had never known him do before, just as a street-bred child might enjoy them on his first day in the country; but of course there was an adjective for everything – 'Monstrous', 'purple', 'grotesque', 'gorgeous', 'curious', 'wonderful' . . . during that day and for many days afterwards he talked of nothing but Reading Prison and it had already become for him a sort of enchanted castle of which Major Nelson was the presiding fairy [sic]. The hideous machicolated turrets were already turned into minarets, the very warders into benevolent Mamelukes and we ourselves into Paladins welcoming Coeur de Lion after his captivity.

And again it was evident that he was regaining a sense of humour. To Ada Leverson, from the Hôtel Sandwich in Dieppe later that day, Wilde wrote: 'I am staying here as Sebastian Melmoth – not Esquire but Monsieur Sebastian Melmoth. I have thought it better that Robbie should stay here under the name of Reginald Turner, and Reggie under the name of R. B. Ross. It is better that they should not have their own names.'

Other friends also had to be thanked for their support. To Mrs Bernard Beere he wrote: 'Worse things might have happened to your old friend, dear, than two years' hard labour – terrible though they were. At least I hope to grow to feel so. Suffering is a terrible fire; it either purifies or destroys; perhaps I may be a better fellow after it all.' And to Frank Harris he wrote tactfully declining the offer of a motoring holiday through France ('Conversations with Frank,' Oscar told Robbie privately, 'are like one long rugby scrum'). But almost as soon as he arrived in Dieppe Wilde was visited by Lugné-Poë, the distinguished French actor who had staged *Salomé* during his imprisonment, and Oscar took this, correctly, as a sign that the French establishment were prepared to overlook his past, granting him that immunity which they habitually reserved for the artist.

The English residents of Dieppe were however otherwise inclined, and their continuing hostility succeeded in getting Oscar slung out of a number of restaurants and cafés where their patronage was too important to be disregarded by the French proprietors. Eventually the sub-prefect of the district wrote Oscar advising him that 'any irregularity of conduct' would result in his expulsion not only from the town but also from the country, and Oscar realized that he would have to seek a more secluded home elsewhere.

He found it a few miles away at Berneval-sur-mer, where he took rooms at the Hôtel de la Plage on 27 May, just a week after his release. By now Reggie and Robbie and More Adey had returned to their own London lives, leaving Oscar alone to cope with his exile. At first he threw himself back into work, writing a long and intelligent letter to the *Daily Chronicle* campaigning for prison reform in general and the reinstatement of Warder Martin at Reading in particular. In his mind Robbie Ross was now safely established as the one true friend ('St Robert'), but already there are references in his letters to love lyrics being sent him by Bosie. 'Absurd' is Oscar's first reaction, but it was to be the opening move in a reconciliation which, when it came, was as swift and as violent as the hatred which had inspired *De Profundis*.

In the meantime Oscar moved from the hotel to a more economical chalet nearby, and there he stayed until the beginning of September, even making vague plans to build himself a house at Berneval one day. Money, though constantly referred to in the letters, was evidently not yet a crippling problem, thanks largely to the £800 that Robbie had been able to salvage from the estate, and Oscar was now full of plans to sell *A Florentine Tragedy* and 'The Ballad of Reading Gaol' just as soon as he could get them finished.

But there were other things to occupy Oscar's mind at Berneval that summer, not least the arrangement of a bizarre little ceremony to mark the diamond jubilee of Queen Victoria, one of the three women (along with Bernhardt and Lily Langtry) that Oscar always said he would have liked to marry:

My fête was a huge success: fifteen gamins were entertained on strawberries and cream, apricots, chocolates, cakes and sirop de grenadine. I had a huge iced cake with 'Jubilé de la Reine Victoria' in pink sugar just rosetted with green, and a great wreath of roses round it all. Every child was asked beforehand to choose his present and they all chose instruments of music . . . they stayed from 4.30 to seven o'clock and played games: on leaving I gave them each a basket with a jubilee cake frosted pink and inscribed, and bonbons. They seem to have made a great demonstration in Berneval-le-Grand, and to have gone to the house of the Mayor and cried 'Vive Monsieur le Maire! Vive la Reine d'Angleterre! Vive Monsieur Malmoth!' I tremble at my position.

There was also a new friendship to cultivate: that of the poet Ernest Dowson, who came to stay and was soon being congratulated on his 'dark hyacinth locks' in letters not so very unlike those Oscar had once written Bosie. Nervous of the way things were going, Dowson took Oscar to a brothel in Dieppe. The visit was not a success, but Oscar told Dowson to spread the word in England that they had been – 'for it will enormously restore my character'.

But Oscar was now almost past caring about his 'character', and freed at last from having to worry about his reputation he began to slip easily back into his former life. Good deeds, such as sending money to clear the fines of some boys in Reading gaol, and hard work on the 'Ballad' still left him with a great deal of spare time. Friends occupied much of that time – apart from Robbie and Reggie, Will Rothenstein, Charles Ricketts and Charles Wyndham all went to see him, and there were joky speculations about whether or not a sinister stranger seen on the beach one day could be a detective paid by Queensberry to make sure that Bosie was not around. Wilde told Gide, another visitor, that the local priest had offered him a permanent seat in church and that he would of course be staying at Berneval forever. Another visitor was the publisher Leonard Smithers, who agreed to take the 'Ballad' as soon as it was complete, and whose dubious private life appealed hugely to Oscar ('He loves first editions – especially of women; little girls are his passion').

But ever and always, in the back of Oscar's mind, there was Bosie; by 2 June, only a fortnight after his arrival in France and less than three months after his completion of De Profundis, Wilde was again writing to 'my dear boy', and it was soon clear that all the efforts of Robbie Ross, Constance, and Lord Alfred's mother to keep the two apart were doomed. Still, Oscar did manage token resistance to Bosie's first suggestion of a meeting: 'Of course I love you more than anyone else. But our lives are irreparably severed, as far as meeting goes. What is left to us is the knowledge that we love each other, and every day I think of you, and I know you are a poet, and that makes you doubly dear and wonderful.'

By 6 June, Oscar was writing to Bosie about the need to ration their letters to one a week rather than the present one a day, and by 15 June they had planned a meeting at Berneval. News of this reached London, however, and two days later Oscar was nervously cancelling the plan, having received a warning letter from his solicitor which Oscar took to mean that Queensberry would intervene yet again rather than let his son fall back into what he still regarded as Oscar's evil clutches. But Oscar now tried to pretend to Robbie that the whole idea of a meeting had been Bosie's alone, and that he would have nothing more to do with it. In the meantime there was still Dowson to keep him amused, and there had been good news from Charles Wyndham, who promised a generous advance if Oscar would buckle down to a new comedy. Worse news came from Carlos Blacker, who wrote in July that Constance was suffering from the creeping spinal paralysis that was to kill her within a year. There were also new financial worries to cloud this late-summer period in which he completed the first draft of the 'Ballad'.

Once what he called 'the quality' had left Dieppe at the end of the summer season, Reggie Turner decided it would be safe to visit Oscar once again without having to fear for his allowance, but after he left Oscar could not withstand the temptation of Bosie any longer, solicitors or no solicitors. They met at Rouen on

28 August, and Bosie later recalled: 'The meeting was a great success. I have often thought since that if he or I had died after that, our friendship would have ended in a beautiful romantic way. We walked about all day long arm-in-arm or hand-in-hand and were perfectly happy. Next day he went back to Berneval and I returned to Paris, but we had settled that when I went to Naples about six weeks later he was to join me there.'

Back at Berneval (which he was now describing as 'dreadful: British weather and all so boring I nearly committed suicide last week') Oscar revised the 'Ballad' which was to be his last completed work and which he now hoped to sell to the *New York Journal* for £200. But he yearned for his next meeting with Bosie, to whom he now wrote:

My only hope of again doing beautiful work in art is being with you. It was not so in old days, but now it is different, and you can really recreate in me that energy and sense of joyous power on which art depends. Everyone is furious with me for going back to you, but they don't understand us. I feel that it is only with you that I can do anything at all. Do remake my ruined life for me, and then our friendship and love will have a different meaning to the world.

Everyone was indeed furious, not least Robbie, who had worked so hard to start Oscar on a new working life after prison, and Constance, who soon threatened to cut off his allowance. Though he knew she was now seriously ill, Oscar could not forgive her for making no effort to reunite him with his sons, and her opposition to Bosie seemed just one more unreasonable and high-handed gesture towards a husband for whom she evidently no longer much cared. But Oscar had been through his £800 at Berneval, and in order to get to Naples and Bosie he was forced to borrow from the journalist Vincent O'Sullivan, who reckoned that his 'loan' (Oscar's usual term for a gift by then) was one of the few things he could look back on with satisfaction: 'It is not every day that one has the chance of relieving the anxiety of a genius and a hero.'

With O'Sullivan's money Oscar joined Bosie at Aix, and they travelled to Naples by train, staying there for a fortnight at Bosie's expense before going on to the Villa Giudice at Posilippo, which Bosie had rented for the autumn. 'When people speak against me,' Oscar wrote to Robbie in September, 'for going back to Bosie, tell them that he offered me love, and that in my loneliness and disgrace I, after three months' struggle against a hideous Philistine world, turned naturally to him. Of course I shall often be unhappy, but I still love him; the mere fact that he wrecked my life makes me love him.'

Robbie was not impressed, Reggie Turner was livid and Robert Sherard spread the news around so that it soon reached the ears not only of Constance but also of Bosie's mother, who similarly threatened to cut off all money supplies immediately unless the two men would agree to part once and for all.

For a while Oscar and Bosie held out at Posilippo against all threats of sanctions from the women; they even found the money to hire four servants for the villa, and to spend a few days on Capri, where they lunched with another exile, Axel Munthe. But after the initial warmth of their reunion the relationship seems to have withered in the chill of autumn, as each man realized that he could not recapture the past. Bosie put it best: 'He has been sweet and gentle and will always remain to me as a type of what a gentleman and friend should be . . . but I have lost that supreme desire for his society which I had before, and which made a sort of aching void when he was not with me.'

Their eventual parting was precipitated by Bosie's mother, who offered him enough money to pay for the rental of the villa, plus another £300 for Oscar as the Queensberry family's share of his court costs, provided Bosie agreed to leave at once and alone for Rome. Bosie did just that, while Oscar stayed on at the villa trying to win his own way back into the affections of all those he had infuriated by his stay with Bosie. Yet their time together had not been totally wasted: Oscar finished his last draft of the 'Ballad', and taught himself that his love for Bosie now had to be considered in an altogether different and less powerful light. At first, he tried to pretend to Robbie Ross that the whole thing had been an aberration, despite the fact that only a week or two earlier he had been writing thundering attacks on the 'interference' of his friends and pointing out that Bosie was no worse than they were in his sexual habits, while remarking acidly that if he were simply living with a Neapolitan renter there would have been no complaints from London at all.

Now however Oscar changed (as was his wont) to an altogether different tack, and told Robbie that Bosie, 'that gilded pillar of infamy', had run off without him once the money showed signs of drying up. It was an unfair and untrue letter, but by then Oscar's only hope of funds lay in reinstating himself in the affections of his London friends, in the hope that they would see him through what he himself now began to think of as his last years.

There were of course still other projects: a play for George Alexander, a libretto for *Daphnis and Chloë*, a poetic drama about the Pharaohs. None of these came to completion and Oscar's only publications after leaving prison were the 'Ballad' and his letters on penal reform, though he did also organize the appearance in book form of *An Ideal Husband* and *The Importance of Being Earnest*.

Oscar did not stay long at the villa after Bosie's departure. He went first to Sicily, to stay with a German baron, Von Gleoder, whose hobby was the photography of naked Sicilian youths; then he returned to Naples for a while, where he found Eleanora Duse at the theatre and begged her to do *Salomé*, an appeal she declined. From Naples Wilde went to Paris, where he was in February 1898 when Smithers eventually published the first six thousand copies of 'The Ballad of Reading Gaol'.

Protected by its anonymity (Wilde had been determined to bring it out under the 'C.3.3' byline, his reasoning being that a little mystery never hurt an author's sales – 'Half the success of Marie Corelli is due to the no doubt unfounded rumour that she really is a woman'), it attracted glowing reviews in the English Press, except from the ever-intransigent W. E. Henley.

Oscar was now less than three years away from his death, and in Paris he at last found himself a home – not in the architectural sense, since he was still to be found lodging in whatever hotel could stand his private life and his inability to pay most bills, but in the sense of a place where he could feel totally relaxed and happy. He rallied for one last letter on penal reform to the *Chronicle* in March, when the Prison Reform Bill was having its second reading in the Commons, but even this he signed simply 'the author of the "Ballad of Reading Gaol" '. Beyond that he was happy to spend his time drifting into a gentle absinthe-tinted decline, no longer driven by the urge to complete any work, or retrieve a reputation about which he had long since ceased to care socially or artistically.

Pictures of Oscar in this last phase of his life show a chubby, faintly seedy boulevardier, a successful publican, perhaps, now fallen on hard times, but able to maintain some appearances and evidently having a ball in so far as he was still young enough, fit enough and wealthy enough to do so. At first Oscar stayed at the Hôtel de Nice, and there picked up boys like Maurice Gilbert ('He grows dearer to me daily and we now dine at a restaurant for two francs'); thirty other lads are mentioned in Oscar's letters from Paris, but none had the fidelity of Maurice who, to his everlasting credit, was one of the few mourners at Oscar's funeral.

But Wilde soon moved from the Hôtel de Nice down the Rue des Beaux-Arts to the smaller, cheaper and infinitely more amenable Hôtel d'Alsace, which was to become his Paris lodging until the day he died. It was there, April 1898, that news reached him of the death of Constance at Genoa, but his grief, though loudly exclaimed to all friends and in telegrams to Robbie in London, was the grief of the past, and it did not long keep him from a life of present Parisian pleasure. There was never much money, but friends could always be touched for a little, and there were cafés where the bills could be left for a week, a month, a year before the proprietor turned nasty.

In the winter of 1898, by which time Beardsley too had died, and Oscar must have been thinking he would yet outlive them all, Frank Harris sent him to Napoule on the Riviera, where Oscar was gratified to notice the size of their bills until a nasty row developed about who was actually to pay them. But by now he was openly admitting that 'something within me is killed ... I feel no desire to write' though that did not prevent him continuing the conversations which made Harris so eager for his company – and which Frank was later to recall with more invention than accuracy in a series of books and articles.

While he was on the beach at Napoule one afternoon, Oscar noted in some amusement that George Alexander passed him on a bicycle, 'gave me a crooked, sickly smile and hurried on without stopping'. Alexander later had the grace to be embarrassed by his own behaviour and, on account of it, agreed to send Wilde £20 a month out of the proceeds of the two plays he had bought from Oscar at the time of his trials. In his will Alexander then left the rights in both plays to Vyvyan Holland, thus eventually redeeming his behaviour towards Oscar once and for all.

Frank, as usual, had been late in arriving at Napoule, but Oscar was unperturbed, largely because in his first few days there he had managed to round up not only 'a beautiful person called André with wonderful eyes' and 'a little Italian called Pietro, like a young St John', but also 'le petit Georges' and an old friend from Paris 'who is like a very handsome Roman boy, dark and bronzelike with splendidly chiselled nose and mouth'. Harris, when he did eventually arrive, thus had to share Oscar not only with half the renters in town but also with Harold Mellor, described by Oscar as 'my new friend', who subsequently took him to his home at Gland in Switzerland after the row with Harris about the hotel bills. 'I hope to be happy there,' wrote Oscar to Robbie of his move to Gland. 'At any rate there will be free meals, and champagne has been ordered, though the Nice doctor now absolutely forbids me to take any on account of gout.'

On his way, Oscar stopped at Genoa to visit Constance's grave. He found it 'very tragic seeing her name carved on a tomb – her surname, my name, not mentioned of course – just "Constance Mary, daughter of Horace Lloyd QC" and a verse from Revelations. I brought some flowers. I was deeply affected – with a sense, also, of the uselessness of all regrets. Nothing could have been otherwise, and Life is a very terrible thing.'

The stay with Mellor was not a success. Oscar decided he liked the villa and the village but now didn't much care for his host, who had turned out to be 'a silent, dull person, cautious and economical: revolting Swiss wines appear at meals: he is complex without being interesting: has Greek loves, and is rather ashamed of them; has heaps of money, and lives in terror of poverty; so I regard it as a sort of Swiss *pension* where there is no weekly bill.'

Soon Oscar was plotting how to escape from Mellor and get back to Genoa, where he had spotted a young actor he quite fancied. Intrigues of one kind or another much occupied him at this time, amorous and financial alike: one plot was concerned with selling his family's Moytura fishing lodge and getting the money over to France before his creditors heard of it, and there is a kind of resilient jollity in his letter-writing which suggests either real happiness or at the very least a placid acceptance of his now nomadic, sponging, petty-pilfering life.

Having escaped Gland and somehow got his hands on some extra money from Robbie, Oscar took himself off on a little tour of Italy, before returning to Paris at the end of May. By now there was news that his brother Willie, too, had died – an alcoholic death, at forty-six – but if the bells were tolling for him too he seems

not to have heard them any more clearly than usual. He picked up his Parisian
life precisely where he had left it: cruising now around the streets, as often as not
in the company of Reggie or Bosie or even Robbie, over on one of their periodic
visits from London, picking up likely boys and looking to others to settle the
accounts wherever possible. His letters at this time concern money and boys,
almost exclusively and always in that order, though in December he was able to
write gratefully to the Lewis Wallers who, in England, had revived *A Woman of
No Importance* only to be greeted by a deafening Press silence.

Early in 1900 there were more deaths to consider. Oscar's Berneval friend
Ernest Dowson and his old enemy Queensberry both died in the first two months
of the year, both (like Beardsley) deathbed converts to Catholicism. Oscar restrained himself from commenting personally on the death of the Marquis, though
he was delighted to notice a week or two later that: 'Bosie is over here [in Paris]
with his brother. They are in deep mourning and the highest spirits.'

In March the friendship with Mellor was patched up, and he and Oscar set off
for Rome where, Oscar later told Robbie:

To the terror of all the Papal Court I appeared in the front rank of the pilgrims in
the Vatican and got the blessing of the Holy Father – a blessing they would have denied
me. He was wonderful as he was carried past me on his throne, not of flesh and blood
but a white soul robed in white, and an artist as well as a saint – the only instance in
History if the newspapers are to be believed. I have seen nothing like the extraordinary
grace of his gestures, as he rose, from moment to moment, to bless – possibly the pilgrims,
but certainly me ... I was deeply impressed, and my walking stick showed signs of
budding.

Such blessing did not however restrain Oscar from picking up 'Armado, a very
smart, elegant young Roman', to say nothing of his friends Arnaldo, Omero and
the other renters for whom Oscar had a few lire and a great deal of time. Photographs of him taken in Rome show a still sturdy, bowler-hatted tourist, a Dublin
businessman, perhaps, in his late fifties on his first Roman holiday. Aside from the
fact that Oscar was a poet in his middle forties they give no cause for concern
about the health that was to desert him so abruptly six months later.

On his way home to Paris, Oscar stayed briefly with Mellor at Gland, and was
taken for his first ride in a motor car, which he found 'a nervous, irritable, strange
thing'. Back in Paris he went to the Great Exhibition and met up with several
local celebrities, including Esterhazy (the spy in the Dreyfus affair) and the young
Serge Diaghilev. He also succeeded in extracting hard cash from Frank Harris, in
return for the outline of a play (*Mr and Mrs Daventry*) which he had already sold
to Alexander and various other managements. Oscar suffered no pangs of guilt
whatsoever (indeed the last letter he ever wrote is a stern defence of this action),
and had evidently convinced himself that it was precisely what Frank would have
done himself if the chance arose.

Now however there were demands even from the proprietor of the Hôtel d'Alsace for payment, and then on 11 October there was a sudden telegram to Robbie Ross in London. It read simply: 'Operated on yesterday. Come as soon as possible.' Robbie arrived within the week to find that the operation had been on the ear Oscar had injured in prison, and that worries about how he was to pay for it were, in the doctors' view, keeping him from a full recovery. Robbie came up with some money, as did Bosie, and for a while their friend seemed to rally – enough, at least, to notice that he was dying, as he had always lived, beyond his means. 'Besides,' he had told Bosie a few months earlier, 'if another century began and I were still alive, I don't think the English could stand it.'

But another century had started, and Oscar had seen almost the whole of its first year. The headaches which had forced him to have the operation now got worse, but Mrs Willie Wilde was in Paris with her new husband, and as Reggie Turner was there too Robbie felt free to travel on to the Riviera, where he had promised to see his mother settled at Menton. Before he left Paris, he warned Oscar that the doctors had said he would not live more than another three months unless he laid off the absinthe, and Oscar made one of his usual promises to reform. On the eve of Robbie's departure however he broke down and wept, convinced that they would never meet again.

That was 12 November; fourteen days later Reggie Turner, who had stayed at the bedside, wrote to Ross with the news that 'doctors now give very little hope of Oscar's recovery', and two days later he was delirious. By the time Robbie got back to Paris, Oscar was dying, having received extreme unction – a deathbed convert to Catholicism. Ross joined Turner in the hotel, and another day passed. That night, as Robbie later told More Adey:

We were called twice by the nurse, who thought Oscar was actually dying. About 5.30 in the morning a complete change came over him, the lines of the face altered, and I believe what is called the death rattle began, but I had never heard anything like it before; it sounded like the horrible turning of a crank, and it never ceased until the end. His eyes did not respond to the light test any longer. Foam and blood came from his mouth, and had to be wiped away by someone standing by him all the time. At 12 o'clock I went out to get some food, Reggie mounting guard. He went out at 12.30. From 1 o'clock we did not leave the room; the painful noise from the throat became louder and louder. Reggie and myself destroyed letters to keep ourselves from breaking down. The two nurses were out, and the proprietor of the hotel had come up to take their place; at 1.45 the time of his breathing altered. I went to the bedside and held his hand, his pulse began to flutter. He heaved a deep sigh, the only natural one I had heard since I arrived, the limbs seemed to stretch involuntarily, the breathing came fainter; he passed at 10 minutes to 2 pm exactly.

It was Friday, 30 November, just six weeks after Oscar's forty-sixth birthday. The official cause of death was listed as an intercranial complication of middle-ear disease.

But that is surely not how Oscar would like his story to end. The images that he had so carefully sustained over the years, first of the dedicated poet and playwright, then of the misunderstood martyr and finally of the carefree playboy, were not supposed to reach their climax in a sordid, messy death. How much better, then, to think of him saying to Reggie Turner: 'It's the wallpaper or me – one of us has to go,' or else telling Robbie Ross: 'When the last trumpet sounds, and you and I are couched in our purple and porphyry tombs, I shall turn and whisper "Robbie, dear boy, let us pretend we do not hear it".'

And the future was, despite everything, to be Oscar's. Although his funeral was a sad and sparsely attended affair, and although he was to lie for nine years in the temporary grave at Bagneux where Robbie and Reggie and Bosie had buried him on 3 December, his rehabilitation as a playwright came faster than even he could have hoped or expected.

Salomé had a triumphant production in Germany in 1902, *De Profundis* was published three years later, and in 1909, spurred by the success that Wilde's plays were having in translation on the Continent and by the consequent discharge of his debts, Ross was able to get his body moved to a permanent grave in Père Lachaise, under a monument graced by an Epstein sphinx. The British Press obituaries had of course been dismissive, even Max Beerbohm's, but within twenty years of Oscar's death as many biographies had been published. All four major comedies had received West End revivals by 1914 (*The Importance* . . . was back in London by January 1902), and although bitter quarrels broke out between Douglas and Ross as to who had been the 'true friend' of Oscar, even these only served to keep his name alive. Bosie actually took Arthur Ransome to court in 1912 for suggesting that it was he who had ruined Oscar, and Ross in turn took Bosie to court later, only to have his own homosexuality established publicly in a way which echoed horribly the events of 1895.

Ross died in 1918, Ada Leverson in 1933, Reginald Turner in 1938, Robert Sherard in 1943 and Alfred Douglas in 1945. But Oscar lived on: by 1975 there had been two films, a one-man show and at least four plays based on his life as well as screen versions of six of his works and countless other radio and television adaptations.

'Let England,' said Lord Alfred Douglas in 1937, 'bear the responsibility for what she did to Oscar,' and at least it cannot be said that England has borne her responsibility in silence. Somehow, one suspects that silence is what Oscar would most have dreaded.

Since this book was first published, interest in Oscar has been sustained by the classic Richard Ellmann biography (1987). In the year of this reprint, 1997, three before the Wilde centenary, we have had Simon Callow's revival of the Micheál Mac Liammóir *Importance of Being Oscar* and a Manchester and London revival of *Lady Windermere's Fan* as well as another in Chichester. In this same year Stephen Fry became the third actor (after Robert Morley and Peter Finch) to play Oscar on the wide screen, in Julian Mitchell's new film adaptation of the Ellmann biography.

ACKNOWLEDGMENTS AND SELECT BIBLIOGRAPHY

No writer of an Oscar Wilde biography in the 1970s can afford to ignore the fact that there have already been more than a hundred books all dedicated to Oscar's life and/or his work and most published since 1920, which averages out at roughly two a year. To read them all would require an adequate knowledge of most European languages and almost unlimited time and patience, and I cannot pretend to have studied carefully more than about one in three. I have however been guided in my reading by the opinions of such authorities as Lewis Broad and Rupert Croft-Cooke, and have found myself referring whenever in doubt to the two acknowledged classics in the field, Hesketh Pearson's *The Life of Oscar Wilde* which has been generally available to all Wilde writers since 1946, and Rupert Hart-Davis's masterly edition of *The Letters of Oscar Wilde* which has only been available since 1963 and was what ultimately made me think there would be room for yet another Wilde biography, since a great many of the references in previous ones can now be proved, disproved or simply sorted out by checking with Oscar's own correspondence.

On these and all the following books I have drawn for something, be it direct quotation, indirect background material or simply an alternative point of view against which to clarify and defend my own. These, then, are the books that have been consciously and intentionally used while I was thinking about or writing mine, and to the author and publisher of each and every one I am most grateful.

There have been other books, too, some long forgotten, others only remotely linked to the subject but all of which have conditioned in some way my views on Wilde and his work, and to their authors and publishers I am no less grateful. It is no coincidence, and it would have greatly delighted Oscar himself, that it is almost impossible to read anything at all about late Victorian society or its theatrical manifestations without thinking sooner or later about Wilde.

In particular I am indebted to the Estate of Hesketh Pearson for permission to quote from *The Life of Oscar Wilde*, to Mrs Vyvyan Holland, Sir Rupert Hart-Davies and Granada Publishing Limited for allowing me to quote from *The Letters of Oscar Wilde*, to Methuen and Co. Ltd for permission to quote from *De Profundis* and to Mr H. Montgomery Hyde and William Hodge and Co. Ltd for permission to quote from *The Trials of Oscar Wilde* in the *Notable British Trials* series. 'The Arrest of Oscar Wilde at the Cadogan Hotel' is quoted by kind permission of Sir John Betjeman, John Murray (Publishers) Ltd and Houghton Mifflin Company from *John Betjeman's Collected Poems* (1958).

Beerbohm, Max, *A Peep Into The Past*, 1972.
  More Theatres, 1969.
Behrman, S. N., *Portrait of Max*, 1960.

Betjeman, John, *Collected Poems*, 1960.

Broad, Lewis, *The Friendships and Follies of Oscar Wilde*, 1954.

Cecil, David, *Max*, 1964.

Connolly, Cyril, *The Evening Colonnade*, 1973.

Croft-Cooke, Rupert, *The Unrecorded Life of Oscar Wilde*. 1972.

De Vere White, Terence, *The Parents of Oscar Wilde*, 1967.

Donaldson, Frances, *The Actor-Managers*, 1970.

Douglas, Lord Alfred, *Oscar Wilde and Myself*, 1914.

   Oscar Wilde: A Summing Up, 1940.

Ellman, Richard (ed.), *The Artist As Critic*, 1970.

Ervine, St John, *Oscar Wilde*, 1951.

Fido, Martin, *Oscar Wilde*, 1973.

Gide, André, *Oscar Wilde, A Study*, 1905.

Harris, Frank, *Oscar Wilde*, 1938.

Hartnoll, Phyllis (ed.), *Oxford Companion to the Theatre*, 1957.

Holland, Vyvyan, *Son of Oscar Wilde*, 1954.

   Oscar Wilde: A Pictorial Biography, 1960.

Hyde, H. Montgomery, *The Trials of Oscar Wilde* (*Notable British Trials* series), 1960.

   Oscar Wilde: The Aftermath, 1963.

Irving, Laurence, *Henry Irving, The Actor and His World*, 1951.

Jullian, Philippe, *Oscar Wilde*, 1969.

Lewis, L., and Smith, H. J., *Oscar Wilde Discovers America 1882*, 1967.

Mac Liammóir, Micheál, *The Importance of Being Oscar*, 1963.

   An Oscar of No Importance, 1968.

Mason, A. E. W., *Sir George Alexander and the St James's Theatre*, 1935.

Matlaw, Myron, *Modern World Drama*, 1972.

Nicoll, Allardyce, *A History of English Drama*, V, 1967.

Osborne, John, *The Picture of Dorian Gray*, dramatization, 1973.

Pearson, Hesketh, *The Life of Oscar Wilde*, 1954.

Ransome, Arthur, *Oscar Wilde*, 1912.

Russell Taylor, John, *The Rise and Fall of the Well-Made Play*, 1967.

Sherard, Robert, *The Life of Oscar Wilde*, 1906.

Stanford, W. B., and McDowell, R. B., *Mahaffy*, 1971.

Stokes, John, *Resistible Theatres*, 1972.

Stokes, Leslie and Sewell, *Oscar Wilde*, 1937.

Wilde, Oscar, *A Critic in Pall Mall*, 1919.

Wilde, Oscar, *Critical Essays*, ed. Ellman, 1969.

Wilde, Oscar, *The Letters of Oscar Wilde*, ed. Hart-Davis, 1963.

Wilde, Oscar, *Complete Works*, 1966.

ILLUSTRATIONS

INDEX